Managing Global Business Strategies: A twenty-first-century perspective

JOHN MCMANUS,
DON WHITE
AND
NEIL BOTTEN

Chandos Publishing

Oxford · England

Chandos Publishing (Oxford) Limited
TBAC Business Centre
Avenue 4
Station Lane
Witney
Oxford OX28 4BN
UK
Tel: +44 (0) 1993 848726 Fax: +44 (0) 1865 884448
E-mail: info@chandospublishing.com
www.chandospublishing.com

First published in Great Britain in 2008

ISBN:
978 1 84334 390 5 (paperback)
978 1 84334 391 2 (hardback)
1 84334 390 8 (paperback)
1 84334 391 6 (hardback)

© J. McManus, D. White and N. Botten, 2008

British Library Cataloguing-in-Publication Data.
A catalogue record for this book is available from the British Library.

Typeset by Domex e-Data Pvt. Ltd.
Printed in the UK and USA.

Printed in the UK by 4edge Limited - www.4edge.co.uk

Managing Global Business Strategies

Southampton
SOLENT
University

MOUNTBATTEN LIBRARY
Tel: 023 8031 9249

Please return this book no later than the date stamped.
Loans may usually be renewed - in person, by phone,
or via the web OPAC. Failure to renew or return on time
may result in an accumulation of penalty points.

ONE WEEK LOAN		

CHANDOS
BUSINESS AND MANAGEMENT SERIES

Chandos' new series of books are aimed at both managers and academics. They have been specially commissioned to provide the reader with an authoritative view of current thinking. If you would like a full listing of current and forthcoming titles, please visit our website, **www.chandospublishing.com**, or contact Hannah Grace-Williams on e-mail info@chandospublishing.com or telephone number +44 (0) 1993 848726.

New authors: we are always pleased to receive ideas for new titles. If you would like to write a book for Chandos, please contact Dr Glyn Jones on e-mail gjones@chandospublishing.com or telephone number +44 (0) 1993 848726.

Bulk orders: some organisations buy a number of copies of our books. If you are interested in doing this, we would be pleased to discuss a discount. Please contact Hannah Grace-Williams on e-mail info@chandospublishing.com or telephone number +44 (0) 1993 848726.

Contents

List of figures and tables

Figures

Tables

About the authors

Dr John McManus writes, teaches and consults in global strategy, technology innovation and leadership. He may be contacted through the publisher.

Dr Don White was dean of business and law at the University of Lincoln (2001–2008). He previously held management positions at the University of Sheffield and Sheffield Hallam University, where he initiated and managed projects with major external corporate clients including LloydsTSB, Northern Foods and Express Dairies. He is a non-executive director of the Lincolnshire NHS Primary Care Trust in the UK. Dr White may be contacted at dwhite@live.co.uk.

Neil Botten is principal lecturer in strategic management and teaches on the MBA and MA programmes at Westminster Business School. His publications include the widely acclaimed *Competitive Strategies for Service Organisations*, co-written with John McManus, and *Management Accounting – Business Strategy and Strategic Supply Chain Management*, co-written with David Harris. Neil acts as a consultant on scenario planning to a wide variety of both public and private organisations. He may be contacted at neil@nabfuture.com.

Acknowledgements

The authors would like to thank those who have given their love and support throughout the process of writing this book.

List of acronyms

ABB	Asea Brown Boveri
A&D	aerospace and defence
ASEAN	Association of South-East Asian Nations
BRIC	Brazil, Russia, India and China
CEE	Central and Eastern Europe
CEO	chief executive officer
CIS	Commonwealth of Independent States
CRM	customer relationship management
EADS	European Aeronautic Defence and Space Company
ERP	enterprise resource planning
ETNO	European Telecommunications Network Operators' Association
EU	European Union
FDI	foreign direct investment
GDP	gross domestic product
GE	General Electric
GNP	gross national product
HAL	Hindustan Aeronautics
ICT	information and communications technology
IPO	initial public offering
ITOL	Information Technology Online
L	light
ML	mid-light
MNC	multinational corporation

MNE	multinational enterprise
MRO	maintenance, repair and overhaul
NAFTA	North American Free Trade Agreement
OEEC	Organization for European Economic Cooperation
OECD	Organization for Economic Cooperation and Development
PEST	political, economic, societal and technological
PESTO	political, economic, societal, technological and organisational
P&G	Proctor and Gamble
PPP	purchasing power parity
PSV	packaged software vendor
R&D	research and development
RoI	Republic of Ireland
RPK	revenue passenger kilometre
SAIC	Shanghai Automotive Industry Corporation
SBU	strategic business unit
SFI	Science Foundation Ireland
SMEs	small and medium-sized enterprises
SOE	state-owned enterprise
TNC	transnational corporation
TQM	total quality management
UNCTAD	UN Conference on Trade and Development
VIVACE	value improvement through a virtual aeronautical collaborative enterprise
VLJ	very light jet
VoIP	voice-over-internet protocols
WGC	wholesale generating company
WTO	World Trade Organization

Introduction

Managing Global Business Strategies is written from a research perspective, and attempts to define and address some of the theoretical and practical issues faced by organisations and their managers in today's business environment. In writing this text the authors draw extensively from their combined international business experience, and where appropriate provide examples to substantiate conceptual points made within the text.

While globalisation remains a central theme, the authors recognise the theoretical limitations within the contemporary global business model and discuss the emergence and situational presence of new business paradigms, such as open business models. The broader comparative framework used allows the observant reader to make strategic connections on political, economic, social and technological levels. While much of the subject matter is grounded within a European business model, the growing presence and influence of Asian and Indian multinationals within the global economy are acknowledged and debated.

While this book is intended to be a learned text, it has been written with a strong emphasis on making sure it is appealing, readable and accessible to executives and practising managers. The applied approach means it should also appeal to business academics and researchers.

Overview of book chapters

The make-up of the book is as follows. Chapter 1 provides the framework for the rest of the book, drawing on a range of contemporary issues to analyse the complex relationships between firms and global markets. This chapter will discuss the ways in which firms have evolved and how they will need to evolve in the future to handle the complexity of doing business in an international and global knowledge-based economy.

Chapter 2 focuses on the role of technology innovation, research and development, marketing and entrepreneurship. The chapter examines and discusses business and strategic practices between continents and countries such as North America, Europe, China, India and South-East Asia. It also looks at the competitive forces that shape international business in a changing global economy. Chapter 3 focuses on the sociological and political climate that is shaping global business by examining how countries and firms undertake business and decision-making in multicultural business environments. The chapter assesses the strategic risks involved in doing business in these multicultural environments. Issues associated with managing cultural diversity will also be examined.

The fourth chapter draws on contemporary research on the theme of global strategy. A number of cases are developed to demonstrate the principles of strategy formulation and examine the inherent strengths and weaknesses in different strategies.

Chapter 5 discusses a number of emergent strategies based on theoretical research and contemporary models. The chapter seeks to reinforce the significance of understanding strategy from a contextual view, and more importantly explores alternative ways in which the business models of a firm can be made explicit. Chapter 6 builds on Chapter 5 by discussing the strategic process using a four-stage model that involves conceptualising, engaging people, articulating the strategy and implementing the strategy by translating it into action.

Overview of case studies

The book contains two case studies, examining the potential of developing countries in two quite different industries – both of which, however, have global importance and can significantly affect the economies of the nations involved. The software industry is not location dependent and services can be delivered anywhere in the world at the press of a key. By contrast, the aerospace industry is highly operational and location dependent, and components are shipped around the world for final assembly.

The first case study, Chapter 7, discusses the global software industry. The world software industry and associated markets are estimated to be worth US$1.1 trillion, with 90 per cent of the world's exports in software coming from the USA and Europe. Evidence would suggest that outside these nations, the new and emerging countries within the software industry are Brazil, Russia, India and China (known as the BRIC nations). Although figures vary, these emerging markets currently account for around 6 per cent of global exports, and the software industry greatly affects the economic systems of these countries. While 'lower-cost labour' is the most commonly cited reason for offshoring, intense global competition in an environment of slower growth and low inflation demands constant vigilance over costs. Due to low costs and high quality, using offshore resources in selected countries seems to make good economic sense. Beyond the cost incentive, global sourcing provides several other practical benefits, including the ability of multinational organisations to stage all-year-round operations efficiently; the opportunity to customise products and services to meet local needs; and the means to deploy workers and facilities geographically to succeed in globally dispersed, highly competitive markets. This case study examines some of the issues within these emerging countries and the effects on the wider global software industry.

The second case study in Chapter 8 evaluates the commercial aerospace industry of the BRIC nations. The aerospace industry has for many years been the province of Western manufacturers, which have exported their products across the globe. This dominance has arisen because of the high requirement for design, engineering and manufacturing expertise essential for these products.

The leading manufacturers estimate that the market for commercial aircraft between 2003 and 2020 will be worth $2 trillion at current prices. The global industry is known to be highly cyclical and tied to both the health and the profitability of the airline industry. Over the next 20 years Boeing predicts that there will be a demand for 25,000 new aircraft, Airbus predicts 16,500 and Rolls-Royce, the engine manufacturer, estimates 41,000. The apparent contradiction in these figures arises because each manufacturer has different products suitable for different segments of the market. Additionally, there is uncertainty about the demand for business aircraft – a significant market for the Brazilian manufacturer Embraer – which may represent up to a third of the demand. This case examines some of the issues within these emerging countries in the wider global aerospace industry.

The rapid change in international and global business

Globalisation of management

The renowned anthropologist Margaret Mead (1970) reiterated a point she had first made in the *New York Times* in 1969: 'we are living in times of change without precedent'. This, she said, explains in part why our children do not regard their parents or grandparents with the respect that ancestor-worshipping cultures did in other places and at other times. Those cultures, living perhaps for centuries in surroundings that hardly changed, could pass on to their children the wisdom of experience and help them cope with most events in their lives. We who did not grow up street-smart in recent times, intimately confronted by drugs and crime, can hear our children say: 'What do you know about growing up today?' In other words, what can you teach us that we need to know?

The comparison for global business is the challenge of managing in times of change without precedent. One of the early pioneers of corporate operational research, Melvin Hurni, observed as long ago as 1955 that one of the truly significant trends in business was the increasing tendency for introspection. Recent trends in global operations towards lean manufacturing and lean business practices define this introspection about business processes themselves. For evidence we can look at the number of firms that have embarked upon business process re-engineering with spectacular success: General Electric (GE), Coca-Cola, EMI, Microsoft, Western Wireless Corporation, Infosys Technologies and the MITRE Corporation, to name but a few. Those who attend prestigious management seminars point out that whereas the old rule of competition was to 'provide the most value for least cost', the new one is to 'do the same in the least elapsed time', minimise the cycle time (velocity) of the entire business and overwhelm your competitors with speed and variety. At the time of his retirement as CEO of GE, Jack Welch was overseeing a corporation that employed 300,000 people in 15 major businesses, from gas turbines to credit cards. Although GE is a complex, wide-ranging company, Welch (2005) always advocated that it must run with the speed, informality and open communication of a corner store. Responding to cyclical business patterns and global business threats with the speed and informality of a corner shop requires great agility and management capability akin to entrepreneurship. Today's global managers and chief executive officers (CEOs) are expected to possess entrepreneurial qualities beyond those of judgement, perseverance and knowledge of the world and business. Above all, global managers must be innovators and supply ingenuity on demand. Executives like Jeff Immelt at GE and Sam Palmisano from IBM are typical global leaders and role models of today.

There is some evidence to suggest that every major country is more preoccupied internally, and less focused on global management, than was the case a decade ago. Enormous changes are taking place in the world of business, whether it is the rise of China and India (McManus et al., 2007a) or the decline of Europe. International finance has become more complex. Not only do global managers have to contend with the vagaries of global finance, but they have to work with a huge range of labour, environmental, legal, ethical, social and governance issues for which many are ill equipped. This is emphasised by the Sarbanes-Oxley Act of 2002, introduced in the USA in the aftermath of Enron,[1] which has done little to turn the tide of governance scandals. The real issue facing many of today's global leaders is what to infer about corporate governance when the rules and expectations of society are changing so quickly. What do you teach managers about the global competitive landscape when countries like China and India are fundamentally changing the rules of the game?

If any one thing characterises the last decade, it has been lost opportunity and crisis management. There was a time when leaders of big multinational firms thought about some governance of the global economy – the principle being that there was no such thing as world government, and national governments in the main were particularly focused on their own jurisdictions when creating the rules of trade and finance or environmental protection of labour. According to William Holstein (2005), firms were moving into this vacuum tentatively, but the world would be run more according to business and market principles. Over the past decade most global managers have decided this was not to their liking; in turn they have created a vacuum into which governments are moving, for better or worse.

Returning to the theme of global management, Aristotle taught that genuine leadership consisted of the ability to identify and serve the common good. To do this requires much more than technical, quantitative or scientific training.

It requires an education in moral reasoning, which must include components of philosophy, literature and logic. Many of the issues facing global firms (and their leaders) are infinitely more complex than they were a decade ago. Most issues facing CEOs are questions of judgement. What looks like a straightforward financial decision to invest in India (to cut costs) by relocating services has implications downstream that cannot be squeezed into an equation. The point is that strategic decisions go awry when based purely on numbers. It is no coincidence that competitive (that is, winning) firms and the people who work for them place significant value on qualitative as well as quantitative capabilities. Such qualitative capabilities include emotional intelligence, in that the more managers understand themselves and their motives, the better equipped they will be to lead in a global world, especially a world where political elements are at work. Political competency means understanding the interplay of policy goals and power goals; political systems are critical to leader effectiveness in a global workplace. It also means an understanding of the geographical and economic implications of political actions. This may require an understanding of different governmental structures and decision-making processes across borders (Goldsmith et al., 2003). Simply being an international business person spells neither political competency nor international competency.

Globalisation of international business

According to Jack Welch (2005), business is like any game. It has players, a language, a complex history, rules, controversies and a rhythm. Learning the rules of the game can take a lifetime, and rewards and profits can seem elusive. Playing and winning the game involve strategy and strategic choices (hopefully good choices, about people, investments and other resources). Defining and implementing a winning strategy require insight, a sense of perspective and courage. Asking the question 'how do we win?' forces firms to define their strengths and weaknesses. It also forces managers to question their own part in the game and how they will play in the competitive field.

According to Peter Drucker (1992), the first true measurement of a company is its standing in its markets. Is its market standing going up or down? And is the improvement in the right markets? The essence of globalisation is to bind markets, performance and profitability into a seamless entity. Welch understood this concept when in 1981 he became CEO of the most complex enterprise in the world. Welch's global mission then was to be number one or number two in the markets in which GE was competing. If this was not feasible, GE's strategy was to disengage and use its global resources to leverage profitability in other markets. During his tenure Jack Welch presided over phenomenal change and increased GE's market value by billions of dollars over two decades. He helped to modernise GE by emphasising a shift from manufacturing to services. In the 1980s GE was not alone in its endeavours to shift its operations into services: in the last five decades we have witnessed a major evolution in Western Europe from being manufacturing-based to being predominantly services-based. There are a number of explanations for this switch. As industrial societies become richer, they choose to spend a higher proportion of their incomes on buying services rather than physical goods. Second, as countries become wealthy, they are able to export their profits in the form of investments in other countries. Evidently, a number of wealthy countries have invested in manufacturing in developing countries (for example, China and India have benefited immensely from foreign direct investment – FDI). The rewards are generally returned in profits, interest and dividends that can be spent on leisure and other services. Thirdly, for many European countries it has proved very much harder to draw out additional productivity from primary and secondary industries such as agriculture and primary processing.

Exchange between nations has grown steadily since 1950. In 2005 GDP (at purchasing power parity – PPP) reached $61 trillion (World Bank, 2005). Since 1990 world trade has increased at a faster rate than world output. This indicates that countries have developed a greater inclination to trade goods and services with one another. Trading nations are today more dependent on each other and on international, multinational and global firms that are directly involved in foreign trade; those that are indirectly dependent on it have become vulnerable to changes in world conditions (Tables 1.1 and 1.2). While many firms are subject to global competition, the trend towards a single global economy is continuing at an accelerated rate. Geographical distance is no longer a barrier between nations; however, the challenges of ethnic diversity in domestic markets are multiplied by the difficulties of delivering goods and services into global markets with different cultures and languages. For instance, demographically by 2010 only 20 per cent of the UK workforce will be white able-bodied males under 45 years of age – consider the resource and cultural implications for firms and managers responsible for delivering global goods and services. Now more than ever organisations have to appraise the wider socio-economic, operating and environmental factors affecting how their goods and services will be delivered.

Table 1.1   Leading exporters in world merchandise trade, 2004

Rank	Exporter	Value ($ billion)	Share (%)	Annual % change, 2003–2004
1	Germany	912.3	10.0	21
2	USA	818.8	8.9	13
3	China	593.3	6.5	35
4	Japan	565.8	6.2	20
5	France	448.7	4.9	14
6	Netherlands	358.2	3.9	21
7	Italy	349.2	3.8	17
8	UK	346.9	3.8	13
9	Canada	316.5	3.5	16
10	Belgium	306.5	3.5	20

Source: World Trade Organization (2004)

Table 1.2   Leading importers in world merchandise trade, 2004

Rank	Exporter	Value ($ billion)	Share (%)	Annual % change, 2003–2004
1	USA	1,525.5	16.1	17
2	Germany	716.9	7.6	19
3	China	561.2	5.9	36
4	France	465.5	4.9	17
5	UK	463.5	4.9	18
6	Japan	454.5	4.8	19
7	Italy	351.0	3.7	18
8	Netherlands	319.3	3.4	21
9	Belgium	285.5	3.0	22
10	Canada	279.8	2.9	14

Source: World Trade Organization (2004)

Undertaking business in a foreign country poses a novel set of problems. For instance, even with advanced data communications firms often have difficulties in obtaining intelligence and competitor information when moving into new business domains or environments. Although market deregulation within North America, Europe and Asia has led to a renaissance in global trade, it has also led to a resurgence of protectionism.

The prophet of globalisation, Kenichi Ohmae (former head of McKinsey's in Tokyo), offered a theoretical argument for the need to become global. Ohmae (1990) argued that firms which have the right characteristics to become global players will succeed only if they operate in three geographical centres of the world (namely the USA, Asia and Europe). Those that stay in just one or two of these areas are unlikely to succeed in the long run, because the loss of economic benefits for those competitors that do not penetrate the total trio will give immense cost advantage to those that do. The argument is based on the fact that these areas contain around one-fifth of the global population in the largest and most sophisticated markets in the world. At the time of making this statement Dr Ohmae had not factored the growing importance of China or India into the equation. Ohmae's belief that size is no bar to globalisation finds an ally in Ferris (1998), who states that 'the late twentieth century may be remembered in the history of science as the time when particle physics, the study of the smallest structures in nature, joined forces with cosmology, the study of the universe as a whole'. Put in business language, the bigger the world economy, the more powerful its smallest players. The resurgence of smaller businesses competing with global and multinational firms is being fuelled by advances in data communications and government policies which favour hungry entrepreneurs with agile approaches to doing business who are not risk-averse.

Already 60 per cent of US exports are created by companies with 20 or fewer employees. Interestingly, John Nesbitt (1994) sees all firms heading in the direction of Microsoft, essentially a peer network of individuals who communicate directly with the CEO.

Global capital and capital markets

In the first half of the twentieth century, those countries (such as the USA, the UK, Germany and France) with access to natural resources such as coal, oil and gas became rich and tended to stay rich. With higher GDP, more capital was saved and subsequently invested, raising productivity and generating more wealth. In the current climate, although still important, natural resources have to a degree fallen out of the competitive equation, as have sources of capital. Historically, international capital markets have allowed residents of different countries to pool risks, imposed discipline upon governments and allowed countries with very little domestic savings to borrow abroad so that they could pursue growth policies. Obstfeld and Taylor (2004) analysed the historical development of global capital markets, employing quantity and price evidence to measure capital mobility during the classical gold standard, the inter-war gold standard, the Bretton Woods[2] period and the recent float (1973–present). Using a new macro-database assembled from primary and secondary sources, they examined PPP, the correlation of savings and investment, covered interest parity and real interest rate convergence. Obstfeld and Taylor (ibid.: 354) found that global capital market integration has followed a U-shaped pattern since the outbreak of the First World War. Integration peaked during the classical gold standard period and declined during the inter-war period, only to recover during Bretton Woods. They noted that market integration has increased dramatically in the last 20 years, and concluded that net flows of foreign capital are no larger today than they were during the classical gold standard period. They note that there are winners and losers from globalisation, and it is very difficult to quantify the costs and benefits of open capital markets.

A recent report prepared by the Japanese Ministry of Economy, Trade and Industry (the Ministry of International Trade and Industry until 2001) highlighted that many of today's industries are far more dependent upon brainpower than on natural resources or capital (METI, 2001). Advances in technology have made access to capital and capital markets easier, and firms have become more sophisticated in leveraging value from their global investments. Improved data communications and technology mean that firms can borrow in London, New York or Tokyo, or wherever the best deal happens to be.

Knowledge capital and the knowledge economy

It is now conventional wisdom among many CEOs that future growth in world trade and investment lies in the nation-state's ability to leverage knowledge capital. Knowledge (and innovation) is increasingly perceived as the means by which global firms secure competitive advantage. With the ease of access to information on a worldwide scale, driven by the internet, globalisation is increasing, and with it the nature of competition and firms being in direct competition with one another. Decomposing organisational hierarchies to leverage knowledge capital requires firms to change on an unprecedented scale. Such change may be achieved not by forming a larger single entity, but by forming loose associations of enterprises that will benefit from the skills of other members of the grouping. The increased knowledge that individuals are able to access will bring about changes not only in the nature of firms and the way that people choose to work and are by definition managed, but also in the way they view firms. Post-Enron the public persona of multinational enterprises is changing. Public demand for good governance and ethical management is increasing and reputations need to be managed.

Knowledge capital is also changing markets, as their sheer size and structure have impacts on governments and nation-states. As knowledge becomes the key resource (of the twenty-first century), it will be increasingly difficult for nation-states to gain competitive advantage using traditional resources. It is likely that governments will have to operate in an increasingly cooperative manner with business, as technology increases the mobility of individuals and deregulation becomes more widespread. Future government policies will need to focus on the development of human capital, the development and nurturing of an entrepreneurial climate and the promotion of broad access to skills and competencies – especially the capability to learn. This will include global firms (and their nation-states) engaged in providing broad-based formal education, establishing incentives for firms and individuals to engage in continuous training and lifelong learning, and improving the matching of labour supply and demand. What flexible firms need most from education systems is not so much investment in the production of skilled but narrowly defined specialists, or in vocational training, but much more investment in the production of people with broad-based problem-solving skills and the social and interpersonal communication skills required for teamwork, along with the skills and attitudes required for flexibility (Oman, 1996: 37).

Foreign direct investment and economic integration

Though multinational enterprises (MNEs) are to be found in almost all countries, their activities are heavily concentrated among wealthy nations. Traditional economic models explain the geographical concentration of economic activity by location of demand, by factor and transport costs, and by economies of scale in production. These approaches imply that, for non-negligible transportation costs, production will often be located near sites of demand and first-mover advantages – that is, in rich countries. The new knowledge-based industries represent, in many ways, a limiting case for the traditional economic model. The software industry, for instance, takes advantage of data and satellite communications which render transportation costs almost zero. Moreover, scale economies are low. There is today a global pool of highly skilled professionals around the world working at markedly lower labour costs than in many of the G8 nations. The growing economic stature of the so-called BRIC nations – Brazil, Russian, India and above all China – means they are emerging as competitors to the USA, Europe and Japan. For example, technical education and advances in infrastructure development have made India the most prominent model of the emergence of a new industrial centre for software development and innovation. India, like China, has benefited immensely from billions of dollars in FDI – see Table 1.3.

Rubens Ricupero (2003), UNCTAD Secretary-General, said: 'in the globalizing world economy, developing countries see foreign direct investment as a factor that can contribute to their long-term economic development. It can be especially important for its potential to transfer technology, create jobs, raise productivity and enhance exports.' FDI is defined as 'a long-term investment by a

Table 1.3 FDI in China and India

	2003 ($ million)	2004 ($ million)	2004 as % of gross capital formation
China			
Inward investment	53,505	60,630	8.2
Outward investment	−152	1,805	–
India			
Inward investment	4,269	5,335	3.4
Outward investment	913	2,222	1.4

Source: UNCTAD (2005)

foreign direct investor in an enterprise resident in an economy other than that in which the foreign direct investor is based'. For many years FDI was dominated by the USA, which accounted for around three-quarters of new FDI (including reinvested profits) between 1945 and 1960. Since that time FDI has spread to become a truly global phenomenon, no longer the exclusive preserve of OECD countries. FDI has grown in importance in the global economy, with FDI stocks now constituting over 20 per cent of global GDP (Hill, 2001).

The FDI relationship consists of a parent MNE and a foreign affiliate which together form a transnational corporation[3] (TNC). FDI has increasingly been viewed as a catalyst to economic growth, particularly in developing countries such as China and India, which have become the most-favoured destinations for FDI. FDI today is seen as a principal conduit for the transfer of technology, know-how and management skills; besides supplementing capital flows into developing countries, it contributes to economic growth and wealth creation. In order for the FDI to materialise, the MNEs must possess some firm-specific competitive advantages that allow them to compete successfully in the foreign environment. These firm-specific assets can relate to production technologies, but they may also be related to special skills in management, distribution, product design, marketing or other links in the value chain, or be made up of brand names and trademarks (Kokko et al., 2001). The theory of FDI stresses the positive links between firm-specific knowledge-based assets and the decision to invest abroad. These assets have some characteristics of supporting a business community and can be transferred at low cost between the MNE subsidiary and its parent company.

The impact of globalisation on countries and companies, especially through increased international competition and opportunities, has enabled investment and outward expansion to take place at a significant rate. According to the *World Investment Report 2006* (UNCTAD, 2006: 26), four factors help explain the drive for internationalisation by developing country TNCs. First, market-related factors appear to be strong forces that push these TNCs out of their home countries or pull them into host countries. In the case of Indian TNCs, the need to pursue customers for niche products – for example, in IT services – and the lack of international linkages are key drivers of internationalisation. Chinese TNCs, like their Latin American counterparts, are particularly concerned about bypassing trade barriers. Overdependence on the home market is also an issue for TNCs, and there are many examples of developing country firms expanding into other countries in order to reduce this type of risk.

Secondly, rising costs of production in the home economy – especially labour costs – are a particular concern for TNCs from East and South-East Asian countries such as Malaysia, the Republic of Korea and Singapore, as well as Mauritius (which has labour-intensive, export-oriented industries, such as clothing). Crises or constraints in the home economy, for example inflationary pressures, were important drivers in countries like Chile and Turkey during the 1990s. However, interestingly, costs are less of an issue for China and India – two growing sources of FDI from the developing world. Clearly, this is because both are very large countries with considerable reserves of labour, both skilled and unskilled.

Thirdly, competitive pressures on developing country firms are pushing them to expand overseas. These pressures include competition from low-cost producers, particularly from efficient East and South-East Asian manufacturers. Indian TNCs, for the present, are relatively immune to this pressure, perhaps because of their higher specialisation in services and the availability of abundant low-cost labour. For them, competition from foreign and domestic companies based in the home economy is a more important impetus to internationalise. Similarly, competition from foreign TNCs in China's domestic economy is widely regarded as a major push factor behind the rapid expansion of FDI by Chinese TNCs. Such competition can also sometimes result in pre-emptive internationalisation, as when Embraer (Brazil) and Techint (Argentina) invested abroad in the 1990s, ahead of liberalisation in their respective home industries. Domestic and global competition are important issues for developing country TNCs, especially when these TNCs are increasingly parts of global production networks in industries such as automobiles, electronics and garments.

Fourthly, home- and host-government policies influence outward FDI decisions. Chinese TNCs regard their government's policies as an important push factor in their internationalisation. Indian firms, on the other hand, have been enticed by supportive host-government regulations and incentives, as well as favourable competition and inward FDI policies. South African TNCs, among others, mention transparent governance, investment in infrastructure, strong currencies, established property rights and minimal exchange-rate regulations as important pull factors. Most importantly, liberalisation policies in host economies are creating many investment opportunities, for example through privatisations of state-owned assets and enterprises.

Apart from the above-mentioned factors, there are two other major developments driving developing country TNCs abroad. First, the rapid growth of many large developing countries – foremost among these being China and India – is causing them concern about running short of key resources and inputs for their economic expansion. This is reflected in strategic and political motives underlying FDI by some of their TNCs, especially in natural resources. Second, there has been an attitudinal or behavioural change among the TNCs discussed in this chapter. They increasingly realise that they are operating in a global economy, not a domestic one, and this has forced them to adopt an international vision. These two developments, along with push and pull factors – especially the threat of global competition in the home economy and increased overseas opportunities arising from liberalisation – add empirical weight to the idea that there is a structural shift towards earlier and greater FDI by developing country TNCs.

The case for China

Researchers Edward Graham and Erika Wada (2001), in a study on FDI in China, make the observation that vast areas of China, including ones where much state-owned industry is located, have not been touched by FDI. In recent years the Chinese government has made FDI promotion a prominent component of its development strategy for the central and western provinces. Although China has strong and flourishing domestic markets built largely by private entrepreneurs, these entrepreneurs are generally regarded as social and political enemies, even though they are very successful in generating income, employment and taxes. China has sufficient invested resources, but the funds go largely to government-run companies or are invested abroad by the government. The typical SME in China gets about 10 per cent of its working capital financing from banks. China's legal and political structures make it difficult for private businesses to flourish, and even though there is a huge banking sector, private firms in China are among the most dependent in the world on internally generated capital.

China's partial reforms, while successful in increasing the scope of the market, have so far failed to address much inefficiency in its economy. If Chinese firms are to compete with the best Western firms they need to improve their financial strength by exporting less capital reserves abroad and investing more in start-up firms and research and development.

In terms of inward investment and export success, China's main advantage for the future is the presence of a clear government strategy for its industries (especially software). However, the geographic dispersal of inward investment is something that many people do not understand, including Chinese officials and Western economists. For example, Zhang Shengman, a Chinese Ministry of Finance official and managing director at the World Bank, argued that China 'must strive for a more desirable distribution of capital flows, both geographically (more to the interior) and sectorally (more to some service sectors, retailing, banking, insurance, etc.)' (Office for South East Europe, 2004).

The case for India

India is characterised by its propensity towards high-skilled, low-cost labour (wages are approximately one-eighth of those in the USA). For example, the Indian software industry began with a strong emphasis on 'body shopping' – the transportation of software staff to work overseas at the client's site. In the late 1980s around 75 per cent of export earnings came from this mode of operation. By 2005 the figure had dropped to around 58 per cent, indicating a slow but steady trend towards offshore working. Having sustained phenomenal growth over the last decade, India is now looking at further opportunities within the global markets (especially in software) to sell added-value services. India's software industry is moving towards the higher end of the value chain that runs from the supply of programming services to providing complete turnkey projects, making it a direct competitor to US and European companies. One of the most critical considerations for the Indian software industry is that the low-cost business model might lose its effectiveness when China's next generation of English-speaking computer science graduates enter the market. This in part explains why there has been a strategic shift by Indian software firms towards the higher end of the value chain.

Software aside, the main forces behind internationalisation are also a direct threat to other products and services offered by Indian firms. As more global firms set up and expand their operations in India the demand for export products and services will diminish, hence India's strategy must be to look to markets outside Europe and the USA – perhaps China and other South-East Asian countries. To sustain its future global market position India will need to tackle a number of issues, including its dependence on the US and European markets and its future access to low-cost working and venture capital.

It is easy to argue that Indian firms will continue to gain market share if they have only a small share of the global market (say 6 per cent), but it is different to suggest the same if India's market share is high (say 15 per cent). India can still gain market share because of cost arbitrage; it is, however, no longer so easy because the impact of the macro environment is much higher. Given this situation, the underlying market strategy seems to be to build scale to meet a rise in outsourcing in the long term, primarily from global telecoms which have yet to embrace the Indian offshore model fully. Evidence would also suggest that many large Indian companies are developing expertise in the so-called vertical domain areas because they offer a rise up the value chain into areas of work that are longer term and more lucrative than, say, traditional 'body shopping'. In addition, aggressive attempts have been made by a small number of Indian companies to globalise through acquisition, by setting up overseas development sites or acquiring a 'front-end' marketing capability.

Multinational enterprises and global enterprises

As previously suggested, FDI is the process by which MNEs transfer resources and capabilities to subsidiaries in overseas countries where market opportunities and location-specific resource endowments exist. Research shows that the largest 500 MNEs are spread across the triad economies (of NAFTA, the European Union and ASEAN) – see Table 1.4. Despite enormous efforts towards restructuring, increased trade and investment opportunities, most of the BRIC nations have an important economic lag and untapped FDI potential.

Globally there is a need for concerted policy efforts to increase competitiveness for FDI within the enlarged BRIC nations. Decisive will be the role of MNEs and host governments, particularly their entry and market development strategies. MNEs, for example, must attain the appropriate

Table 1.4	Top 500 MNEs within triad countries		
Triad	Regional grouping	MNEs	%
NAFTA	USA, Canada and Mexico	198	39.6
European Union	UK, France, Germany, Italy, etc.	156	31.2
ASEAN	Japan, Australia, New Zealand, Malaysia, etc.	125	25.0
Other	China, India and Russia	21	4.2

configuration between their internal resource deployment and the potential opportunities and risks in different countries. This is achieved by ensuring that subsidiaries adapt strategies to both the environmental contingencies of the host country and the resource configuration of the parent company. Within this approach some subsidiaries mainly transfer know-how, skills and technology from their parent in order to operate in the host country; others develop technology, new products and organisational capabilities that contribute to the upgrading of their parent's firm-specific advantages (or benefits). Since different types of subsidiaries contribute differently to the host economy, how corporate headquarters-subsidiary relationships are structured is also a public policy issue for host governments as it directly affects the potential cost-benefit returns to the economy (Table 1.5).[4]

Those MNEs operating outside the triad regions are often faced with additional costs compared to local competitors. These costs are generally associated with cultural, legal, institutional and language differences, lack of knowledge about local market conditions and the expense of communicating and operating at a distance. Therefore, if an MNE is to be successful in another country, it must have some competitive advantage that overcomes the costs of operating in a foreign country or market. Either the firm

Table 1.5   Host-country costs and benefits

Potential costs	Potential benefits
Trade: decrease of relative export to import ratio	Increase in output
Transfer pricing	Increase in wages
Decrease in domestic savings	Increased employment
Decrease in domestic investment	Increased exports
Instability of balance of payments	Increased tax revenues
Loss of control over domestic policy	Realisation of economies of scale
Increase in unemployment	Provision of technical and managerial skills
Establishment of local monopoly	Weakening of power of domestic monopoly
Inadequate technology to support local knowledge and skills	Provision of new knowledge and skills

must be able to earn higher revenues for the same costs, or have lower costs for the same revenue, than comparable domestic firms. In essence it must have some advantages not shared by its competitors. These advantages must be strategic and specific to the firm, and readily transferable within the firm and between countries. Although somewhat over-prescribed, the extent to which an MNE gains leverage is by differentiating its processes and resource allocation and the unique interrelationship that exists between the subsidiary and its host-country suppliers, customers, competitors and government agencies. To emphasise this point, some MNEs have taken advantage of China's reformed economy to enter the Chinese market through alliances and partnership arrangements. Other MNEs that have expanded into China have taken the opportunity to share know-how to tap into the abundant export markets.

The emergence of the global enterprise

For many, globalisation is seen as primarily an economic phenomenon, involving the increasing interaction, or integration, of national economic systems through the growth in international trade, markets, investment and capital flows (Figure 1.1). This integration acts simultaneously, interconnecting and linking processes together. It offers the world a set of new markets, tools, rules and consumers.

The drivers of globalisation are the business managers of large MNEs. But their business strategies are triad-oriented (Table 1.4), in that they are regional and responsive to local consumers, rather than global and uniform. To emphasise this point, the automobile and speciality chemicals industries are triad-based, not global. Global firms, according to Bartlett and Ghoshal (1989), are defined in three ways: the multinational, which operates as

Figure 1.1   Comparison of global enterprises and MNEs (focus and capability)

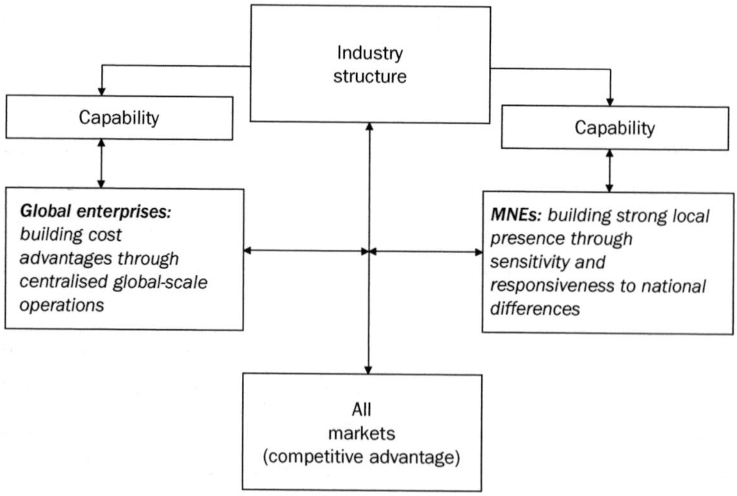

Source: adapted from Bartlett and Ghoshal (1992: 15)

a decentralised federation, emphasising responsiveness to national markets; the international, also a federation but more coordinated at the centre, with emphasis on developing expertise and knowledge on a worldwide scale; and the global organisation, which trades from a central hub and emphasises global efficiency. In many respects, this process of global efficiency limits the capacity of nation-states to manage their territory and requires them to redirect their policies taking into account global networks of information and financial decisions over which they have little or no control. In this sense, the capacity for action of a nation-state will depend upon its capacity for action within globalisation. According to this logic, being competitive will increasingly depend on the capacity to produce knowledge and process huge quantities of information.

Globalisation obviously offers great opportunities and challenges, including opportunities for knowledge, technology sharing and strategic alliances. Increasingly, strategic alliances are seen as a way into global markets, with software firms leading the trend. Some Chinese firms have managed to establish strong international brands through such alliances; for example, the alliance of US firm Computer Associates with NEUSOFT Group (a software company based in Shenyang in north-east China) aims to develop new-generation industrial solutions to serve Chinese customers better. These strategic alliances are usually defined as agreements committing firms to work together towards a shared strategic objective. If successful, such alliances generally develop into joint ventures or long-term collaborations. Strategic alliances are important, and as Jeff Immelt, the current CEO of GE, points out: 'in today's dynamic business environment, standing still is not an option. No matter how large or small, organizations must continue to grow in order to survive, let alone succeed, particularly in light of the recent globalization phenomenon'

(General Electric, 2006). This comment backs GE's goal to have $10 billion in consumer finance assets on the Asian subcontinent by 2010 (ibid.). In August 2005 the head of GE Money claimed to have the equivalent of $1.3 billion in Indian consumer finance assets. GE also plans to make acquisitions to increase growth after 2009, when foreign investment rules for banking investment in India are scheduled to be relaxed (ibid.).

Figure 1.1 emphasises the different strategic attributes and forces that impact on firms. Firms are increasingly required to adopt global and agile strategies to deal with the new realities of doing business. For example, the belief that MNEs develop homogeneous products for the global market and through efficient processes are able to dominate local markets everywhere is simply not the case. In reality, MNEs have to adapt their products for local markets (Rugman, 1996; Rugman and Cruz, 2000).

Global competition in all major markets between firms from all main trading nations within the triad regions, the increasingly multinational origin of the inputs to production of both goods and services, the growing intra-industry (and intra-product) nature of world trade and the interdependent nature of the various elements of globalisation, including entrepreneurship, are all contributing to a transformation of the global economy and global enterprise.

Global and intra-corporate entrepreneurship

Entrepreneurship is often viewed as a function involving the exploitation of opportunities that exist within a market. Such exploitation is most commonly associated with the direction and/or combination of productive inputs. Entrepreneurs are usually considered to bear risk while pursuing opportunities, and are often associated with creative and innovative actions. The traditional view of entrepreneurship involving technological innovation and introducing new or improved products to the marketplace or to the world is characterised by people in business who have the passion to succeed, the ability to innovate and a strong sense of personal integrity. A new renaissance in entrepreneurship is being fuelled by advances in information technology, government deregulation and cheap capital. Brent Hobermann, founder and co-CEO of the pan-European, UK-based Lastminute.com, noted that the growth of funding sources in Europe has made things easier. 'Two years ago, when we were raising money, there were five companies we could approach for seed funding,' he said. 'Six months ago, there were easily a hundred' (quoted in Liss, 2000). Entrepreneurial individuals such as Bill Lynch are creating the new global economy. Lynch[5] built Imperial Holdings into South Africa's largest transport and mobility conglomerate after arriving there in 1971 with just £2,000 and no job. Today Imperial has annual revenues of €6.5 billion across seven synergistic divisions (integrated logistics solutions; fleet management; vehicle and forklift leasing; aviation operations, sales and leasing; car rental and tourism; motor vehicle importation, sales and after-sales services; and related financial services) and employs 36,000 people on three continents.

Much of the new wealth that is being created is associated with four key trends: the dot.com wave; the emergence of global start-up firms; capital-chasing entrepreneurs; and changes in supporting institutions for entrepreneurship in different countries. For example, the dot.com wave has launched new role models and provided a wake-up call for established firms, and has been a catalyst for old-economy start-ups as well. It has also been a catalyst for developing an understanding of entrepreneurial activity outside the USA.

A global perspective

Much of the new export wealth and GDP within the triad regions comes from entrepreneurial activity (Figure 1.2). Over the past three decades service sectors have become an important feature of the world economy, and exports of services in the triad now exceed those of manufactured goods. The growth in entrepreneurial activity within the service sector is phenomenal and includes transportation services; architectural, construction and engineering services; education and training services; banking, financial and insurance services; entertainment; information services; and professional business services. Although the sector has benefited from entrepreneurial activity and innovation, it has come at a price. Successful global entrepreneurs will testify to the fact that they cannot operate in a void. The political, legal and cultural environment directly impacts on their activity and their ability to contribute to the economic development of a country.

Open global markets are vital to entrepreneurship but, surprisingly, the growth in entrepreneurial activity in Europe

Figure 1.2   Comparison of world export and GDP growth, 1951–2003 (1951 = 100)

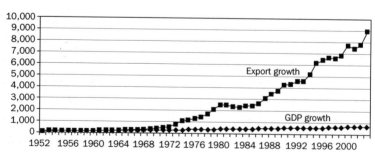

Source: World Trade Organization (2005)

and Asia has been low compared to that in the USA; this is partly due to levels of bureaucracy and the complexity of doing business within nation-states. France, for example, controls access to its markets through sophisticated legal regimes and trade barriers; and although Germany is very receptive to entrepreneurial activity and business innovation it is still burdened by structural problems, including inflexibility and over-regulation in labour markets, taxation and business establishment, as well as high social insurance costs. Clearly, the role governments play is pivotal to developing real political and economic stability in an entrepreneurial society. Entrepreneurs often rely on governments (and other entrepreneurs) to leverage market entry. One principal concern shared by many entrepreneurs is 'aggressive' government policies that slow down innovation and time to market and interfere with reward mechanisms. Aggressive bureaucracy often leads to conflict. The software industry, for example, has some of the greatest global entrepreneurs and innovators in the world, but their vision and success (as in the case of Bill Gates) put them at odds with their national governments. In China, for example, entrepreneurship and innovation have historically been regarded as culturally unacceptable. Research into China's computer and associated software industry reveals the diverse sources of entrepreneurs and the conflicts which can arise from government/state-sponsored entrepreneurship. Although there was some level of entrepreneurship inside the closed Chinese economy before the 1980s, the opening up and creation of private property were fundamental to the transformation of China. According to Williams (1987), China has relied on three types of entrepreneurs: the classical private sector business-owner who manages the firm for his/her own benefit and makes his/her own decisions; collective enterprises which are owned by more than one person and have a relationship with a government supervision agency (yet are fairly autonomous); and the state-owned enterprises, where employees use state resources in an entrepreneurial way by increasing competition and forging linkages with local and foreign enterprises. While the latter two forms created competition and technological learning, they also generated tensions between entrepreneurs and the state bureaucrats, who sometimes saw successful initiatives as a challenge to their control over the economy. While the state was important in the first phases of adjustment, state presence gradually decreased after 1994 as institutions matured. Lu (2001) shows how three of the largest firms in the Chinese electronics industry evolved from collectively owned enterprises which depended on government support for capital for investments, technology and human capital resources. Government support greatly reduced risk during the early growth phases of these companies, which are now seen as leading success stories within China.

An intra-corporate perspective

If entrepreneurship was simply a matter of outstanding ability occasionally fertilised by government funding, the challenge of building a community of entrepreneurs would be relatively simple and straightforward. Yet executives from industry and government describe a far richer and more complex spectrum of enablers. The availability of human talent and cutting-edge research, the regulatory, accounting, legal and capital conditions that facilitate the transition from ideas into wealth-creating products and services, the access to international markets and protection for intellectual property that enable innovators to capture the returns on their investments are all essential parts of the process. Weakness in any of these elements diminishes the others and, indeed, the entire platform for entrepreneurship and innovation.

According to Ian Smith (Oracle's UK MD), innovation is crucial to Oracle's long-term survival. He says: 'young people coming out of education at the moment have very high expectations of being entrepreneurs. They are beginning to learn business skills at school and that is encouraging them to be highly entrepreneurial and to expect to start their own business rather than go into corporations' (quoted in Brown, 2006). Young people under 25 have more in common with half a billion people who are aged under 25 in China and India than do most executives. Most of them are better connected to each other than are the boards of many UK plcs. Oracle's strategy is to create an environment that encourages entrepreneurship (and talent): when an employee has a good idea, they feel that they are starting their own business within the company. This type of intra-company entrepreneurship relies on the firm's ability to integrate and feed investment into its innovation process and markets.

Market orientation is a critical factor in developing focused innovation, and consists of three behavioural components: customer orientation, competitor orientation and interfunctional coordination. It is known that market orientation leads to innovation and entrepreneurial activity in firms. According to Michael Porter (1980), a market-oriented approach to focused innovation relies on an interfunctional analysis of a firm's value chain to determine ways to appropriate additional value. Thus an important aspect of entrepreneurial activity is the ability to understand the various functional elements that make up a process or product. To be successful at focused innovation, firms need to develop intra-corporate entrepreneurs who can draw upon cross-functional teams of people with functional expertise. This theme will be returned to in the next chapter.

Key chapter messages

- Today's global managers and CEOs are expected to possess entrepreneurial qualities beyond those of judgement, perseverance and knowledge of the world and business.

- Not only do global managers have to contend with the vagaries of global finance, but they have to tackle a huge range of labour, environmental, legal, ethical, social and governance issues for which many are ill equipped.

- Demographically, by 2010 only 20 per cent of the UK workforce will be white able-bodied men under 45 years of age, which has resource and cultural implications for firms and managers responsible for delivering global goods and services.

- Although market deregulation within North America, Europe and Asia has led to a renaissance in global trade, it has also led to a resurgence of protectionism. As world markets shrink and countries become more protectionist, the propensity to undertake trade with like-minded countries increasingly leads to blocking out undesirable competitors.

- The resurgence of smaller businesses competing with global and multinational firms is being fuelled by advances in data communications and government policies which favour hungry entrepreneurs with agile approaches to doing business who are not risk-averse.

- It is now conventional wisdom among many CEOs that future growth in world trade and investment lies in the nation-state's ability to leverage knowledge capital.

- It is likely that governments will have to operate in an increasingly cooperative manner with business, as technology increases the mobility of individuals and deregulation becomes more widespread.

- The growing economic stature of the so-called BRIC nations – Brazil, Russian, India and above all China – means that they are emerging as competitors to the USA, Europe and Japan.

- The impact of globalisation on countries and companies, especially through increased international competition and opportunities, has enabled investment and outward expansion to take place at a significant rate.

- China's main advantage for the future is the presence of a clear government strategy for its industries (especially software).

- India, having sustained phenomenal growth over the last decade, is now looking at further opportunities within the global markets (especially in software) to sell added-value services.

- Globally there is a need for concerted policy efforts to increase competitiveness for FDI within the enlarged BRIC nations. The role of MNEs and host governments, particularly in their entry and market development strategies, will be decisive.

- For many business leaders globalisation is seen as a primarily economic phenomenon, involving the increasing interaction, or integration, of national economic systems through growth in international trade, markets, investment and capital flows.

- A new renaissance in entrepreneurship is being fuelled by advances in information technology, government deregulation and cheap capital.

- Open global markets are vital to entrepreneurial growth, but the growth in entrepreneurial activity in Europe and Asia has been low compared to that in the USA; this is partly due to levels of bureaucracy and the complexity of doing business within nation-states.

Notes

1. Often referred to as the first major failure of the 'new economy', the collapse of Enron Corporation stunned investors, accountants and boardrooms and sent shockwaves across financial markets when the company filed for bankruptcy on 2 December 2001.
2. The Bretton Woods system of international monetary management established the rules for commercial and financial relations among the world's major industrial states. The system was the first example of a fully negotiated monetary order intended to govern monetary relations among independent nation-states. Until the early 1970s the Bretton Woods system was effective in controlling conflict and achieving the common goals of the leading states that had created it, especially the USA.
3. Transnational corporations (TNCs), most of them privately owned, undertake FDI. However, in some home countries (notably in the developing world) and in some industries (especially those related to natural resources) a number of major state-owned enterprises are also increasingly expanding abroad. According to estimates by UNCTAD (2006), the universe of TNCs now spans some 77,000 parent companies with over 770,000 foreign affiliates. In 2005 these foreign affiliates generated an estimated $4.5 trillion in value added, employed some 62 million workers and exported goods and services valued at more than $4 trillion.
4. Triad-based MNEs compete for global market share and profits across a wide variety of industrial sectors and trade services.
5. Bill Lynch, CEO of South Africa's Imperial Holdings, was named the 2006 Ernst & Young World Entrepreneur.

2

The market and competitive forces that shape international and global business

Globalisation of markets

Markets of the 1950s and 1980s and all the years in between were characterised by the influence and development of Taylorism,[1] but it is post-Taylorist, flexible forms of entrepreneurial organisations that drive and shape globalisation today. It could be argued that the current wave of globalisation coincided with the Reagan and Thatcher governments of the early 1980s and the emergence of post-Taylorist organisations whose formidable competitive strength constitutes the principal microeconomic force now driving globalisation. The movement of tangible and especially intangible forms of capital, finance, technology and ownership or control of assets has become the most prominent feature of globalisation, while corporate strategies and behaviour (in both financial and non-financial sectors) drive it. Rapid and pervasive technological change, notably in the application of microelectronics, and changes in government policies and market deregulation have visibly shaped and given impulse to a new wave of globalisation since the late 1970s (Oman, 1996).

Equally important is far-reaching change in 'industrial organisation', i.e. the way activity is organised within firms and the way firms cooperate and compete. This change blurs the very distinction between industry and services. More than any other, it disrupts entrenched oligopolies[2] and alters the 'rules of the game' across many sectors worldwide. Many of these new game rules have focused on deregulation and global competition in all major markets (telecommunications, financial services, transportation, etc.) in almost all major countries, the increasingly multinational origin of inputs to the production of goods and services, the growing intra-industry role of world trade and the interdependence of the various elements of globalisation. All are contributing to a transformation of markets and the global economy (see Table 2.1).

In their book *Competing Against Time*, George Stalk and Thomas Hout (1990) argue that the ways in which firms manage and compress time in all their activities are the most powerful sources of competitive advantage. Responsiveness to global and market conditions and giving customers what they want when they want it are key to success. Stalk and

Table 2.1   Characteristics of globalisation

Global characteristic
Time compression is a global competitive weapon
Domestic markets are no longer protected from international competition
A firm's ability to compete globally in all markets is crucial
Size and structure are important in order that firms may roll out their products and services quickly to market
Rapid expansion into major markets now requires outward investment as well as exports
The boundary between markets and hierarchies is shifting, with new forms of functional integration emerging
Emerging labour markets are changing market boundaries
Globalisation of production and sourcing is leading to increasing specialisation across international boundaries

Hout claim that time compression was the fundamental advantage behind Japan's success in a number of highly competitive markets, enabling firms to increase the variety and technological sophistication of their products and services. In the contemporary global business environment, using time-based strategies (new business models and systems approaches to strategy formulation) brings the benefits that accrue from market synchronisation, in that products and services can be brought to market quickly, establishing a valuable lead over competitors.

Some interesting examples can illustrate these characteristics, one being solar cells. Critics of the technology argue that it is not cost-effective and therefore cannot make any headway in the market without huge government subsidies. The sceptics conclude that solar energy is commercially a non-starter, hardly worth the effort. Japan's manufacturers turn this thinking on its head. Like Fujitsu, Honda and Canon in the 1990s, instead of waiting until the price is low enough to promise a market, firms such as Sharp and Sanyo are relentlessly attacking the technology now, in an effort to drive down costs quicker through innovation (*The Economist*, 2005). Many of Japan's high-technology firms are pursuing a similar approach in areas such as robotics and aerospace. One of Japan's largest companies, Toyota, is investing millions in battery/petrol-driven hybrid vehicles as a stepping-stone to fuel-efficient cars and has already begun testing fuel-cell vehicles in America.

Along with Japan, Brazil is making its presence felt in high-technology markets. One firm, Embraer, has become one of the largest aircraft manufacturers in the world by focusing on specific market segments with high growth potential in commercial, defence and executive aviation. Embraer employs around 17,000 people (86 per cent of whom are located in Brazil), and has managed to build a significant market presence by providing competitive and innovative solutions with high technological standards. It uses lean production methods and strategies focused on time compression to market – modern tools which allow Embraer to reduce the development time of any new aircraft. Customers can follow the aircraft development steps and are able to check the internal configuration and define the configuration scheme to exact specifications.

Although Embraer benefited from government intervention in its fledgling years, not all industries have been so fortunate. Brazil's macroeconomic national policies are sometimes dissociated from public efforts to promote market growth, and this has hindered some other high-tech industries. The high value of Brazil's currency in relation to the American dollar for most of the past decade, combined with continuing high interest rates diverting investment away from production and export, has contributed to reducing many local industries' external competitiveness.

External competitiveness to a degree is premised on what you know about your competitors. Too often a firm starts out with a good understanding of its business and markets, but quickly loses touch as the market grows and changes. Customers are often fickle and retention strategies can consume a disproportionate amount of firm resources, but in the long run understanding where your customers come from, what they buy from you and what they could buy elsewhere is vital. Without this knowledge there is no way of knowing and understanding your markets. Customer relationship management (CRM, or old-fashioned customer care) is now considered a major discipline by which many multinational firms benchmark and maintain key customer accounts. William Edwards Deming predicted the usefulness of CRM years ago when he wrote of the need to stay ahead of the customer: 'The customer does not know what he will need in one, three, or five years from now. If you, as just one of his potential suppliers, wait until then to find out, you will hardly be ready to serve him' (quoted in Neave, 2000).

Global expansion of world trade

A big influence on the globalisation of customers to markets has been technology. The rapid expansion in business-to-business and business-to-commerce in the last five years has been breathtaking. As stated in Chapter 1, much of the current expansion in world trade is being fuelled by a renaissance in entrepreneurial activity and innovation. In the past, entrepreneurs were disadvantaged by the buying and bargaining power of the bigger firms. To some extent this situation has been diluted as bigger firms hook up with smaller knowledge-based businesses to leverage economies of scale that were once the domain of the multinational Taylorist producers. In today's global market competitiveness depends increasingly on the coordination of, and synergy generated between, a broad range of specialised industrial, financial, technological, commercial and cultural skills which can be located anywhere around the world. What this translates into is rationalisation. Production is being rationalised globally, with firms combining the factors, features and skills of various locations in the process of competing in markets (Hatzichronoglou, 1996). There are three major dimensions of change involved: increasing national (location) specialisation; increased international fracturing of value chains or chains of production and greater line-item by line-item trade imbalances; and substantial structural dislocation in local, regional and national economies, and a consequent need for major structural adjustment. Faced with these multiple challenges, usually requiring action going beyond the capabilities of any single firm, and even those of *ad hoc* cooperation between firms and governments, it is important (still) to have a comprehensive concept of the goal of competitiveness so as to orientate the search for global competitiveness in different markets.

Reconstructing markets for a new twenty-first-century economy requires considerable motivation on the part of national governments and business to work together in partnerships to enable bureaucracy to be cut and trade to flow. Many economic observers believe that promoting trade (ease of doing business) and economic integration within the European Union has been and continues to be an uphill struggle – according to Klause Krone (quoted in Liss, 2000), 'if we are not enabling government into the change process, we will not be successful in the long run'. While increasing economic interdependence is widely recognised, there is (still) no such general agreement on the shape that the international economic order is to take in response to the pressures that interdependence generates.

From a conceptual point of view, two different broad approaches to deal with increasing economic interdependence can be identified (Bertrand et al., 1999): shallow and deep integration. Shallow integration involves increasing market access consistent with the maintenance of national sovereignty regarding non-border policies. In such a world, countries tend to refrain from incrimination of foreign products or producers, but retain their freedom of action in other areas and compete on the basis of their natural endowments and regulatory regimes ('competition among rules'). With deep integration, governments are willing not only to integrate their economies further through liberalisation but also increasingly to treat domestic regulatory policies and international interactions between policy areas as matters for international coordination, and provide for corresponding delegation of powers. Overall, the international economic order remains closer to the first than to the second model – that is, shallow integration predominates, though not without significant gaps, and the most binding international disciplines are those seeking to improve market access and reduce discrimination. Interestingly Djankov and McLiesh (2005), leaders of the Doing Business project, argue that there is a straightforward, positive relationship between the 'ease of doing business' and the Human Development Index, suggesting that reforms could have a positive and widespread impact in developing economies. They contend that more than two percentage points could be added to the growth of the 'most difficult countries to do business in' if they adopted the regulations that exist in the least difficult ones (ibid.: 3). According to Djankov and McLiesh:

> It takes 153 days to start a business in Maputo, but two days in Toronto. It costs $2,042 or 126% of the debt value to enforce a contract in Jakarta, but $1,300 or 5.4% of the debt value to do so in Seoul. It takes 21 procedures to register commercial property in Abuja, but 3 procedures in Helsinki. If a debtor becomes insolvent and enters bankruptcy, creditors would get 13 cents on the dollar in Mumbai, but more than 90 cents in Tokyo. Borrowers and lenders are entitled to 10 main types of legal rights in Singapore, but only 2 in Yemen. In Nigeria and Senegal the property registration cost amounts to about 30% of the property value. And even when a formal title is well-established, it will not help to increase access to credit if courts are inefficient, collateral laws are poor and there are no credit information systems, because no one would be willing

to lend. Add to this rigid employment regulation, and few people will be hired. Arguably women, young and low-skilled workers are hurt the most: their only choice is to seek jobs in the informal sector.

Some academic researchers into globalisation argue that the economic centre of gravity is shifting from nation-states in the West to those in the East and the southern hemisphere (Govindarajan and Gupta, 2000). Countries such as Singapore, Hong Kong, Thailand and South Korea have secured and strengthened their competitive positions in many market sectors (financial services, electronics, education, etc.). Not surprisingly, the embrace of market mechanisms has allowed the developing economies of the world to start catching up with the advanced economies. The convergence of telecommunications and computers has made possible a global command-and-control structure for transnationals, building a global assembly line for goods and services. In building this assembly line a single management framework has emerged which assimilates many of the management innovations, disciplines and experiences of the last 20 years (TQM, lean manufacturing, business re-engineering, supply-chain management, etc.). Many of the West's Asian competitors have embraced and used these techniques with spectacular success. This view of globalisation requires that all management innovations be thought of as mechanisms to drive up customer value and make the firm more competitive.

Market opportunities for firms operating within the OECD

The increasing global importance of countries operating in the OECD[3] (Organization for Economic Cooperation and

Development – Table 2.2) is reflected in the growing number of European firms that have merged or been acquired in the last five years. Some of the largest mergers and acquisitions within the OECD in recent years have been the record-breaking merger of British Telecom and MCI (telecommunications); Daimler-Benz and Chrysler (autos); DuPont and Herberts (chemicals and paints); Alcatel and Motorola (telecommunications equipment), and Alcatel's subsequent acquisition of DSC Communications; the acquisition of MCA by Seagram (entertainment); and the purchase of Marion Merrel Dow by Hoeschst (pharmaceuticals). The biggest buy-out in history was when Britain's Vodafone/Airtouch took over Germany's Mannesmann for $185 billion in 2000, creating the largest wireless telephone corporation in the world. This new company now controls the biggest Euro markets in Britain, Germany and Italy and has holdings in more than 30 countries, including the USA and Japan. Historically national identities have been a big issue in European takeovers, but although both corporations had strong national identities their respective governments did not intervene. The Vodafone/Mannesmann merger illustrates the propensity to

Table 2.2　　A–Z of countries within the OECD

Australia	Germany	Luxembourg	Sweden
Austria	Greece	Mexico	Switzerland
Belgium	Hungary	Netherlands	Turkey
Canada	Iceland	New Zealand	UK
Czech Republic	Ireland	Norway	USA
Denmark	Italy	Poland	
Finland	Japan	Portugal	
France	Republic of Korea	Spain	

support international profits (and stock prices) over domestic concerns, and underscores how national markets and politics are becoming secondary factors in a globalised economy.

The expanding field of mergers and acquisitions within the OECD illustrates the growing interconnections of a single world capital class – for an analysis of the formation of the transnational class see Robinson and Harris (2000). According to Robinson and Harris:

> the reality of capital as a totality of competing individual capitals and their concrete existence as a class relation within specific spatial confines determined geographically as nation-states worked against a transnational, or supranational, unifying trend in the development of world capitalism. The liberation of capital from such spatial barriers brought about by new technologies, the worldwide reorganisation of production, and the lifting of nation-state constraints on the operation of the global market imply that the locus of class and group relations in the current period is not the nation-state.

Today, the expansion of direct foreign investment, cross-national mergers, strategic alliances, the interpenetration of capital and interlocking directorates that are transnational are all examples. Outsourcing, subcontracting and various licensing agreements have resulted in a 'production chain and complex webs of vertical and horizontal *integration* across the globe' (ibid.) in such a way that it is increasingly difficult to separate local circuits of production and distribution from globalised ones.

According to Dicken (1998: 223), transnational corporations:

> are also locked into *external* networks of relationships with a myriad of other firms: transnational and

domestic, large and small, public and private. It is through such interconnections, for example, that a very small firm in one country may be directly linked into a global production network, whereas most small firms serve only a very restricted geographic area. Such inter-relationships between firms of different sizes and types increasingly span national boundaries to create a set of *geographically nested relationships from local to global scales*... There is, in fact, a bewildering variety of inter-organisational *collaborative* relationships.

Such integration and interrelationships are visible in high-tech industries such as defence and information technology. European corporations like the European Aeronautic Defence and Space Company (EADS, based in the Netherlands) are breaking down barriers to investment in the billion-dollar US defence industry. EADS sold 2,000 helicopters to the US Coastguard, the Border Patrol and the Department of Homeland Security. It is also involved in partnerships with Northrop and Lockheed on government contracts with billion-dollar price tags.

Although the USA is seen by many European TNCs as a major market, firms operating within the OECD have recently sought to increase their presence and investment funds within CEE/CIS regions (Central and Eastern Europe and Commonwealth of Independent States). The majority of companies targeted operate in manufacturing, financial services, energy and utilities industries, as well as the food and beverage sector. A recent report by PriceWaterhouseCoopers (2005) highlights significant activity regarding market opportunities and mergers and acquisitions within the CEE/CIS (Table 2.3). The number of cross-border acquisitions was three times higher than in 2004. One interesting observation made by PriceWaterhouseCoopers is that 56 per cent of all deals in 2005 were domestic

Table 2.3					

Top ten mergers and acquisitions in the CEE/CIS regions in 2005

Rank	Investor	Target	Investor country	Target country	Approximate value (US$ m)
1	Gazprom OAO	Siberian Oil Co OAD	Russian Federation	Russian Federation	13,091
2	Vodafone	Mobilfon SA	UK	Romania	2,500
3	Telekom Austria AG	MobilTel EAD	Austria	Bulgaria	1,969
4	Investor group	Milkhailovsky GOK OAO	Russian Federation	Russian Federation	1,650
5	Market purchase	Mobile Telesystem OAO MTS	Russian Federation	Russian Federation	1,530
6	Telekomunikacja Polska SA (TP SA)	Polska Telefonia Komorkowa Centertel Sp zoo (PTK Centertel)	Poland	Poland	1,508
7	Gazprom OAO	AKS Holding OAO	Russian Federation	Russian Federation	1,386
8	Telefonica SA	Cesky Telecom	Spain	Czech Republic	1,077
9	Conoco Philips	LukOil	USA	Russian Federation	1,062
10	Raiffeisen Zentralbank Oestereich AG-RZB	Aval Joint Stock Post Pension Bank	Austria	Ukraine	1,028

transactions, driven by the Russian domestic mergers and acquisitions market where the rate was 72 per cent. In contrast, Romanian and Slovakian mergers and acquisitions markets are dominated by inward transactions – 72 and

63 per cent respectively, compared to an average 40 per cent for the region.

Russia's new-found status as a global market provider of energy to OECD countries is attracting a significant amount of inward investment; this adds to the domestic money that was parked offshore and has been coming back into the economy in the last two years to be used for capital investment in non-energy sectors like construction, textiles, heavy machinery, food processing, microbiology, pulp and paper and fertilisers. The flow of Russian investment back into the country indicates that Russian managers firmly believe in their country's ability to adapt to new economic realities. Two things helped the Russian economy: higher oil prices, and a devalued rouble that made domestic companies more competitive. Energy sales account directly for about 16 per cent of GDP and a third of government revenues. *Business Week* (2006) recently calculated that every $5 drop in the price of crude costs Russia about 1 per cent of GDP. For the longer term, Russia cannot rely exclusively on energy resource revenues, but must focus on deep institutional reform of its economy. It has made significant strides in the last year, but the country's debt level is still high and much depends on whether Russia is able to adapt to a slowing world economy and lower oil prices. Recent economic intelligence produced by Goldman Sachs (Duncan, 2005) suggests that Russia could become the world's number six economy – ahead of the UK, Germany and France – by 2050.

Global and international service markets

The global importance of service industries is evident from the acquisitions that have been made in these markets.

Strategic acquirers are actively seeking growth opportunities, primarily in financial services, technology, energy and utilities. Some of the key outcome indicators of the globalisation of an industry are the extent of cross-border trade within the industry as a ratio of total worldwide production, the extent of cross-border investment as a ratio of total capital invested in that industry and the proportion of industry revenue accounted for by firms competing in all major regions of the world. While it is acknowledged that there is considerable variation across OECD countries in the extent to which they have experienced rapid development of high-growth service industries,[4] using the relative ratios above one may assert that in terms of cross-border flows many of the OECD's major producing nations – the USA, Japan, Germany, the UK, France and Italy – have significant investments in high-value-added industries such as bioengineering, information and communication technology, pharmaceuticals and automotive technologies. Many of the firms operating in these different market sectors are increasingly reliant on supply chains that embrace an element of physical commodities and tangible services. Both Dell and Wal-Mart are examples of companies that have pulled together production and service to leverage cost, quality and service. The rise in global services and service industries in the last decade might be described as spectacular – following the global depression of the early 1990s many firms retracted and took a hard look at their core business. To quote Jack Welch (2005: 170), 'by the time I was made CEO, I knew that GE had to get as far away as it could from any business that smelled like commodity and get as close as possible to the other end of the spectrum'. Under Welch's leadership GE went on to invest heavily in financial services – GE Capital bought RCA, which included NBC – and transferred resources into utilities and high-value service provision.

In the service economy there are new ground rules, including barriers to both entry and exit. Strong growth in services has occurred in Canada and Australia, two countries with open economies and relatively few regulatory barriers; in contrast, growth in services has been slower in countries like Japan, where the business environment has been less favourable to entry by newcomers and to risk-taking, and where extensive cross-holdings of shares and the strength of relationships have slowed industry restructuring. Services have fundamentally different characteristics from commodities, and these differences have crucial implications for the way the service economy must be organised. Unlike physical goods, many services have an intangible aspect about them which makes them difficult to copy (or pirate), and their consumption value is based on the intrinsic nature of the service being offered to the consumer.

The increasing importance of technology within services industries such as banking and financial services is emphasised by the growing profits and shareholder returns. Within this industry information and communication technology now enables people to participate in a growing number of service-related activities in real, or deferred, time, without having to be physically present (Botten and McManus, 1999). Within many global and international service markets the convergence of e-commerce (and business-to-business) based on internet standards is causing a fundamental shift in the way business operates by creating new markets and new opportunities; as a result, we are now living in a world where global-scale service companies exist for the first time. Global-scale services companies operate in industries such as education, consultancy, health, telecommunications, distribution, retailing, transportation, tourism, entertainment, banking and financial services. Banking, for example, is a mature industry which is going through increasing market turbulence. The industry has long been subject to strong institutional control and protected by high entry barriers, but deregulation and the increasing importance of technology are leading to the deconstruction of these barriers. One-time scale economies are no longer a substantial barrier for new entrants, since successful internet banking is grounded in flexible processes rather than mere economies of scale (Canals, 1999).

As markets change so does the relationship between service providers and consumers, in ways that may have significant implications for economies of the present and future. Not only does technology allow providers to produce a single product which is not mass-produced, it also allows a single product that is capable of being mass-consumed, either on a standardised or a customised basis. Such is the case with online internet access to dictionaries, encyclopaedias, newspapers, museum collections, etc. It will also be the case with key basic operating software in the near future, as both Microsoft and Sun Microsystems have announced their intention to supplement distribution of packaged software with online versions. The software industry has experienced exponential growth on the back of multimedia and home entertainment. As a consequence of economic liberalisation, many of the markets that were once the domain of very powerful countries such as the USA, Japan and Germany have become more accessible. Free trade has become a reality within the major trading blocs of the EU, NAFTA, ASEAN and Mercosur. Low wage inflation and access to skilled labour from Eastern Europe and OECD countries such as Turkey and Poland are enabling countries like the UK to gain stronger competitive positions in many service-related industries.

In terms of globalisation, wage rates and differentials (Gray, 2006: 36) have lured a huge number of businesses to relocate their operations to other countries (Table 2.4), creating service sector jobs where there are growing markets and access to skilled labour. Those countries with low wage rates, especially China, India, Korea and Mexico, are poised to become players in the next 20 years, thus one could assume that the economic centre of gravity is not merely shifting towards the developing countries, but may lie directly in the middle of what we currently regard as the developing bloc. Nations like Korea and Mexico (which incidentally is a major producer and exporter of oil) have the capacity to become significant economic and market leaders in those moderately regulated markets where price is a key differentiator.

To sum up, barriers to trade and investment in and among countries and within markets will hopefully continue to decline in the next decade, fuelling further globalisation.

Table 2.4   **Index of comparative hourly cost of workers, 2004**

Country	Rate	Country	Rate
Norway	150	Japan	95
Denmark	146	Italy	88
Germany	140	Spain	74
Netherlands	133	Greece	53
Finland	132	Israel	53
Switzerland	131	Korea	50
Belgium	129	Singapore	32
Sweden	123	Portugal	30
Austria	122	Taiwan	28
Luxembourg	115	Hungary	25
France	103	Hong Kong	24
USA	100	Czech Republic	23
Ireland	95	Mexico	11

Policy, regulation, consumers and the market

The market and competitive forces that shape international and global business are in many respects tied to domestic policy and regulation. Traditionally, regulation has been designed to deal with perceived market failures, such as externalities related to investment in networks or infrastructure, or asymmetric information between producers and consumers. Studies conducted in Germany (Mannheim Innovation Panel, 1999) highlight that inappropriate regulation makes firms less likely to innovate and adapt the quality and mix of goods and services to changing consumer needs. In recognition of the adverse effects that regulation can have on markets, many of the multinational firms that operate within the OECD (and in other countries such as China and India) have devised strategies and business practices that enable cross-border transactions to take place under conditions that minimise bureaucracy and bureaucratic interventions. The increasing volume of cross-border transactions and interdependence of trade flows, investment, technology and capital create the need for greater coordination and integration of policies relating to them. There is also a requirement for trade (and industry) associations and national governments to work at a higher level of integration which is mutually reinforcing.

Within the information and communications technology (ICT) industry, the European Telecommunications Network Operators' Association (ETNO[5]) has advocated the creation of a level playing field throughout the EU. The main challenge in this context is effectively reducing the regulatory burden and bureaucracy across Europe as competition develops and convergence fundamentally changes the marketplace. Completing the transition to a sector mainly driven by market forces under EU competition law and enabling truly sustainable infrastructure-based competition are essential for increasing the competitiveness of Europe's ICT sector. So far the implementation of the regulatory framework at both European and national levels has led to more regulatory intervention rather than less. The guiding question for the future institutional structure under EU directives should therefore be who would be best placed to achieve these objectives. According to ETNO's FAQ webpage (www.etno.be), in response to the query 'Would a progressive roll-back of regulation create new monopolies and slow down investment in the sector?':

> Initially, regulation was precisely planned to evolve from a monopolistic to an open and competitive sector. Markets have evolved considerably since then. Thanks to new technological developments, competition in the market place will continue to increase. A roll-back of ex-ante regulation would not lead to new monopolies. Firms must be allowed to develop new services and applications together with competitors on commercial terms and not on the basis of continued micro-management by the regulator. A deregulatory trend would encourage further investment by all market players in competing platforms and infrastructures, for the full benefit of consumers.

There is abundant evidence that much can be gained from further regulatory reform in other service sectors, including road, rail and air transport, distribution services, professional services and financial services. Further regulatory reform of the telecommunications industry should provide better access to ICT, such as high-capacity broadband communications, which is of great relevance to many service sectors. More generally, reducing administrative barriers for start-up firms is an important area for reform, since this can promote greater business dynamism and entry (Table 2.5).

Consumers and the market

It could be argued that markets stand apart from much of the human institutional landscape because nobody designed them. Markets are natural orders which pursue no hierarchy of ends; that is, markets do not value certain ends over other ends, like the state does (Blundell, 2006). In this respect markets are a mass of different perceptions and circumstances, a subtle web of individuals, or firms as agents of individuals, trying to guess tomorrow's opportunities and customer needs.

Irrespective of what is meant by globalism, it is the customer who determines what a business is. According to Peter Drucker (1954), there is only one valid definition of business purpose: to create a customer. Because its purpose is to create a customer, any business enterprise has two – and only these two – basic functions: marketing and innovation. They are the entrepreneurial functions. The general ethos of the marketing business process requires that all innovations be thought of as intended to help get and retain customers – in short, to make the firm more competitive. Some of the biggest opportunities for the cultivation and exercise of the marketing process exist today in the service sectors. Deregulation in the financial services sector and the increasing importance of ICT are leading to huge innovations in the banking industry. For instance, the outside venture of Prudential, a leading international financial services company, with Egg (its internet brand) has overcome much of the inherent second-utility nature of financial services by linking them to first-utility

Table 2.5   OECD views on regulatory reform

Sector	View on reforms (based on OECD source information)
Business services	While business services are not as highly regulated as other services, some restrictions do exist, notably in the areas of engineering services, employee recruitment and education In advertising, a remaining issue concerns diverse national regulations governing the kinds of marketing and advertising which are allowed (including controls designed to protect heath, uphold decency and protect privacy)
Distribution services	A wide range of regulations, including restrictions on large stores, opening hours and zoning, appear to have slowed structural change in the sector Regulations have sometimes affected the efficiency of the distribution system, but mostly appear to have limited the range of services provided to consumers
Electronic commerce	Issues related to the development of electronic commerce include rules and regulations regarding consumer protection, privacy, authentication, access to infrastructure and taxation Decisions that are made in these areas will play an important role in determining the overall nature and impact of electronic commerce on economies
Financial services	Where it has occurred, regulatory reform in financial services, particularly greater competition, has resulted in increased productivity, lower costs and prices, and gains from improvements in the quality, variety and flexibility of financial instruments Overall resource allocation has been improved and disruptions to financial flows from swings in macroeconomic conditions have been reduced, while countries have benefited from increased international capital mobility
Network-based content services	Reforms are needed to realise the potential of new services based on digital networks in three interrelated areas: general policy frameworks, including liberalisation of rules governing market structure, ownership and access, and protection of intellectual property rights; regulatory institutions and procedures, particularly licensing policies and commercial codes of conduct; and public support programmes, including efforts to promote domestic content

| Table 2.5 | OECD views on regulatory reform (*Cont'd*) |

Sector	View on reforms (based on OECD source information)
Professional business services	Where restraints on commercial aspects of professional practice have been relaxed, prices are lower and new services are appearing in response to consumer demand, while at the same time maintaining quality, performance standards and consumer protection through entry controls, licensing, etc. Market access restrictions on foreign providers are limiting the ability of service providers to address the needs of clients that are expanding internationally
Telecommuni-cations	Reform to facilitate competition in telecommunications has resulted in lower prices, improved product/service diversity and customer choice, enhanced quality, reduced costs, higher productivity and accelerated network development and modernisation Perceptions that reform would impact negatively on provision of universal service, increase prices and reduce commercial viability of incumbent operators have not been supported by actual experience

Source: OECD (1997)

products such as wine, books, food and drink, CDs etc. Another provider, Security First Network Bank, leveraged the banking industry expertise of Cardinal Bancshares and the technical expertise of SecureWare to sell internet-only financial services, and also to develop secure customer interface software for incumbent banks (Clark and Lee, 1998).

The cultivation of customers in many respects relies on the firm's (and management's) ability to make leaps into the minds, emotions and practices of customers, and into the vulnerabilities of competitors. Some of the biggest opportunities for the cultivation of the marketing and customer interface exist within the service industries. Services have certain unique properties. They can usually be more easily and quickly redesigned and less expensively customised and remanufactured than can process or manufactured tangible products.

Consider how the convergence of new technologies has impacted on e-commerce-led service activities. Recent new entrants within the global banking sector have taken advantage of technology to impose new and disruptive ways of competing on existing incumbents. Those who manage the industry believe the power in the channel of retail financial services is already shifting to innovative new entrants able to offer a more attractive and efficient consumer banking interface.

It could be argued that much of our current thinking on consumer behaviour has been focused on the question of what we know rather than what we should know. Selling to a global market where consumers come from diverse cultures with different tastes requires a locally driven strategy that addresses the unique characteristics of buyers. The new model of management thinking confronts the intuitive principle that a consumer is an extension of a person with an existing and defined identity, who we can understand by getting to know their personal life and circumstances in all of their diversity and richness. Instead it is argued that the twenty-first-century consumer is a subject that continually constructs identities for itself by entering into the process of consumption. In Oswald's (1996) words:

> the subject of consumption is nothing if not an actor in search of an identity... Lacking a basic core identity, the post-modern subject constructs itself around the image it projects for others in consumer culture. 'I am what you perceive me to be.' Consumption enables people to change hats as the occasion demands.

The relationship a consumer has with a brand is continually changing. The meaning of a brand can only be understood in the context of the discourse in which the brand is being consumed and the way the firm markets the brand. Unilever, for example, is one of the largest consumer goods companies in the world. This British-Dutch firm currently makes in excess of 1,000 brands of food and home and personal care products in 158 countries. Much of Unilever's success can be attributed to its high national responsiveness and low economic integration strategy, and its proactive market focus. Unilever's strategy is to remain close to its customers in local markets while giving regional managers authority to make decisions based on local needs and tastes. According to Professor Tian (undated), both consumer behaviour and business practices are conditioned to a large extent by the culture within which they take place. Therefore, in order to match the marketing mix with consumer preferences, purchasing behaviour and product-use patterns in a potential market, marketers must have a thorough understanding of the cultural environment of that market, i.e. marketing cross-culturally. However, this is by no means to suggest that in the twenty-first century all marketers should focus on cultural differences only to adjust marketing programmes to make them accepted by consumers in various markets. In contrast, it is suggested that successful marketers should also seek out cultural similarities, in order to identify opportunities to implement a modified standardised marketing mix. To be able to manipulate these similarities and differences in the worldwide marketplaces skilfully is one of the most important marketing strategies for businesses in the twenty-first century.

Innovation and diffusion

Neil Postman (1993), in *The Surrender of Culture to Technology*, writes about how technology has entered our language and shaped our world view. We have hundreds of new words that stem directly from digital technology: *reprogramming, information highway, internet, software* and *digital* are a few obvious examples. But technology also changes words that already exist, such as *information, news, public opinion, instant* and *community*. These shifts and nuances are silent and less obvious, as indeed are the changes in the meaning of words such as *fact, truth, intelligence, freedom* and *memory*.

So what about the word *innovation*? Innovation could be described as 'the entire process by which new knowledge is generated and diffused into the market'. Innovation in a business and market context often means different things in different industries – be they automotive, food, retail, transport, pharmaceuticals, software, financial services or education. Innovation can be a new product, process or raw material. A firm may choose to compete by developing new products or processes. The success of the Japanese car industry during the latter part of the twentieth century was mostly derived from process innovations (using quality-based methodologies developed by William Edwards Deming and Joseph Juran).

The automotive industry is perhaps a good example of innovation in the new and old economies of the twentieth and twenty-first centuries. Cars best represent the industrial economy of the twentieth century. Today, however, this old industry is systematically linked to the tools and organisation of the new economy, in much the same way that feudal farming was transformed by the industrial revolution. Today there are five automotive transnationals which own or control 20 formerly independent manufacturers. A typical example of global presence is Japan's Mazda building cars in Spain in a factory owned by Ford in Europe. Recent research shows that more than 85 per cent of all automobiles are produced in North American factories owned by Ford,

General Motors, DaimlerChrysler and European or Japanese MNEs (Rugman, 2001).

Abby Cohen, chief strategist at Goldman Sachs, notes: 'In many ways it's artificial to draw a distinction between the so-called new and old economy, because the real magic of the US economy has been the enormous application of innovative technology' (quoted in Harris, 2001). The Schumpeterian theory of 'creative destruction' discusses an economic model wherein innovation is a highly competitive process and dynamism is best captured by small, new firms which continuously displace incumbent firms at the frontiers of technology. Although small firms contribute significantly to their national economies, it is the larger MNEs which power global competition by continuously drawing from their pool of cumulative knowledge and acquired technological capabilities over time. Large firms have superior access to capital and are more able to spread risk. Large corporations like Microsoft are able to invest millions of dollars in innovation and start-ups. At the beginning of this decade almost 86 per cent of new venture capital in the USA went to internet-related companies. Not to overgeneralise the point, small firms in the ICT sector have shown themselves to be more efficient in their use of capital resources in producing innovation.

Circumstances that favour innovation are generated by a mix of factors specific to the nature of the industry and the strategic actions taken within it. By definition, all strategic action represents a dialogue between the firm and its business environment. Firms that operate in a global arena face a series of political, economic, societal, technological and organisational (PESTO) barriers. Firms that seek strategic and market breakthroughs require innovative improvements in management thinking in order to realise their full potential. Barriers such as those listed in Table 2.6 may be

Table 2.6   PESTO barriers and their traits

Barrier	Traits
Political	Inertia Legal Governance Ethics Regulatory Competitive legislation
Economic	Profit Shareholder value Financial justification Market conditions Exchange rates
Societal	Conceptual (visioning) Critical mass (consumers) Opinion and behaviour Public interference Education and skills availability Changes in lifestyles
Technological	Technological feasibility Research and development (R&D) New patents and products
Organisational	Corporate culture Resources Structures Processes

faced by any firm operating within national or global markets. Doing away with barriers is essential for fulfilling the potential of globalisation in promoting the diffusion of ideas, innovative concepts and specialisation on the basis of comparative advantage. This, in turn, can have a positive impact on long-term global growth. There is some disagreement concerning the causality direction between innovation and market growth. Some writers argue that innovative firms are more likely to export, and regress different indicators of innovation on market performance

Table 2.7	Examples of performance measures	
Indicators of generation of knowledge	Indicators of diffusion of knowledge	Indicators of use of knowledge
Number of patents Number of engineers and scientists Mobility of professionals Technological diversity (for example, number of technological fields)	Timing/stage of development Regulatory acceptance Number of partners/ number of distribution licences	Employment Turnover Growth Financial assets

Source: Carlsson et al. (2002)

(Table 2.7). Others argue that exposure to global markets makes firms more innovative. This appears to be a reasonable position to take. Exposure to competitive markets is more likely to force firms to make product and process innovations to meet the demands of global consumers.

Key chapter messages

- The movement of tangible and especially intangible forms of capital, finance, technology and ownership or control of assets has become the most prominent feature of globalisation, while corporate strategies and behaviour drive it.

- In the contemporary global business environment, using time-based strategies (new business models and system approaches to strategy formulation) brings benefits that accrue from market synchronisation, in that products and services can be brought to market quickly, establishing a valuable lead over competitors.

- External competitiveness to a degree is premised on what you know about your competitors. Too often a firm starts out with a good understanding of its business and markets but can quickly lose touch as the market grows and changes.

- Reconstructing markets for a new twenty-first-century economy requires considerable motivation on the part of national governments and business to work together in partnerships to enable bureaucracy to be cut and trade to flow.

- The increasing global importance of countries operating in the OECD is reflected in the growing number of European firms that have merged or been acquired in the last five years.

- Outsourcing, subcontracting and various licensing agreements have resulted in a production chain and complex webs of vertical and horizontal integration across the globe in such a way that it is increasingly difficult to separate local circuits of production and distribution from globalised ones.

- In the service economy there are new ground rules, including barriers to both entry and exit.

- Service industries have fundamentally different characteristics from commodities, and these differences have crucial implications for the way the service economy must be organised. Unlike physical goods, many services have an intangible aspect which makes them difficult to copy (or pirate), and their consumption value is based on the intrinsic nature of the service being offered to the consumer.

- As markets change, so does the relationship between service providers and consumers, in ways that may have significant implications for economies of the present and the future. Not only does technology allow providers to produce a single product which is not mass-produced, but it also allows a single product that is capable of being mass-consumed, either on a standardised or a customised basis.

- The new model of management thinking confronts the intuitive principle that the consumer is an extension of a person with an existing and defined identity, who we can then understand by getting to know their personal life and circumstances in all of their diversity and richness.

Notes

1. Based on the work of Frederick W. Taylor (1911), the global spread and development of Taylorism in the 1950s and 1960s greatly enhanced productivity levels worldwide. But it also laid the foundations for building up, over time, rigidities in production and in the running of large organisations.
2. An economic condition in which there are so few suppliers of a particular product that one supplier's actions can have a significant impact on prices and on its competitors.
3. Established in 1961 to replace the Organization for European Economic Cooperation (OEEC), the OECD is an international body composed of the industrialised market economy countries as well as some developing countries. It provides a forum in which to establish and coordinate policies.
4. The contributions of primary, secondary and tertiary activities to total value added have changed sharply over recent decades. Agriculture, fishing and forestry are now relatively small in almost all OECD countries. The share of manufacturing has also fallen in most countries, while services now account for well over 60 per cent of total GDP in all OECD countries.
5. ETNO, the European Telecommunications Network Operators' Association, was established in May 1992 and has become the principal policy group for European electronic communications network operators.

3

The socio-cultural forces that shape international and global business

Global interaction of cultures and economic systems

In a contemporary twenty-first-century economy, intercultural awareness is the key to international business success. It is estimated that international trade increased from $136 billion in 1960 to approximately $9 trillion at the beginning of this century. Moreover, increasing migration and more business opportunities have produced broader levels of interaction across cultures and business domains. In a world where global brands dominate retail environments in every country, it is evident that we now undertake many business operations in a global economy. Any visitor to an Asian city is greeted by the sight of people wearing Western football shirts, billboards advertising designer-label fashions and local families queuing up for a McDonalds restaurant. The global economy has become one not only of trade but also where cultures and identities are merging. Managers are increasingly exposed to working with or within a multiplicity of business cultures. This involves working in other countries, working in organisations that have a diversity of operations in other cultural environments or dealing and communicating with customers and markets from a wide range of cultures. As John Saee (2007) observed: 'the globalisation of national economies has fuelled the need for intercultural communication. The increase in international trade now far exceeds any single national economy, including major industrialised countries.' Many CEOs and their managers can expect to spend increasing time and energy on understanding and working in different countries and cultures. In essence they will need to educate themselves to do business and manage in this new global context. This presents three key interdependent challenges for CEOs.

- The need to become more interculturally competent in order to operate in an increasingly diversified business world.

- The need to understand and develop business models that will be suitable for this changing context.

- The need to create organisational models and structures which will reflect the new circumstances and gain maximum benefit and opportunity.

So, what are the emerging markets and changes in patterns of activity, and how are these creating new challenges and interdependencies? Many business commentators place great emphasis on the four emerging world economies: Brazil, Russia, India and China. Although located in different regions with different political climates, the sheer size of the BRIC countries, combined with robust growth rates, sets them apart from other emerging markets (Savage, 2007: 32). All the emerging markets across the BRIC nations display one similar characteristic: they all have large and rapid growth rates. The growth has been initiated and is typically dominated by development in the large metropolitan areas where increasing middle-class populations are driving economic demand and change through increased consumer spending on a range of domestic goods. But all four countries have large rural hinterlands and populations where this change is slower to develop. Consequently all four areas have large and increasing wealth disparities between rich and poor. As consumer habits and demand expand from the metropolitan areas into the less developed rural areas, growth will continue to expand in the longer term but it will drive new and different ways to access and market products.

A second tier of emerging markets which demonstrate some similar characteristics to those of the BRIC nations includes Indonesia and Vietnam in Asia, Colombia in Latin America and Ukraine in Eastern Europe. Economic growth in these countries is beginning to drive consumer spending on domestic goods. The size of populations means there is unlikely to be any reversal of this trend. A world expansion of consumer spending is driving the global economy. The global economy is not a new concept, and international or global companies have existed for many years. The British East India Company, founded in 1600, is popularly cited as the world's first international and global company. Four hundred years on, however, it is no longer the case that international business means Western multinational companies selling to or operating in world markets. The rise of Asian and South American economies means that economic flows have become increasingly complex. Hans Ulrich Maerki of IBM observed in 2007 that both capital and trade flows are now increasingly multidirectional: 'the deepening of global trade, capital and information flows, enabled by a flat world, is changing where and how business value is created'. He cites a number of examples, including:

- global investment banks send derivatives processing to Dublin;

- US radiologists send x-rays to Australia for analysis;
- Asian chipmakers use US engineers for expertise;
- Asian clothing manufacturers outsource design to Italian designers;
- customer service centres in Nova Scotia handle warranty enquiries for US shoppers.

Between 2000 and 2003 foreign firms built 60,000 manufacturing plants in China. As discussed in Chapter 1, FDI is now truly a global issue, with export of capital and acquisitions coming from the emergent BRIC nations. For example, the acquisition of the UK's Corus Steel by India's Tata Group in 2006 was followed by a move into automotives through the acquisition of UK-based Jaguar and LandRover. There is now a strong move in China to export capital and make foreign acquisitions, driven in part by state-backed strategies to secure access to increasingly scarce mineral and energy sources essential to continued growth. Much of this trend represents the use of large capital assets by cash-rich Chinese businesses to acquire stakes in the European and US financial sectors. In November 2007, for example, China's second-largest life assurance group paid £1.3 billion to become the top shareholder in Fortis, the Belgo-Dutch banking and insurance group (Waples, 2007). These examples indicate how much more complex and multidirectional the flows of the world economy have become.

Consumer-led growth in the BRIC and other emergent economies is creating powerfully resourced organisations which are moving from being trading partners to being owners of and investors in major Western businesses. The Eastern economies are beginning to take a large and direct stake in the markets and businesses of the West. This major socio-economic shift is leading to an increasing and inexorable interdependence between business managers and owners from different cultures. Working with different cultures is moving from the need to have an understanding in order to promote your business abroad to dealing with a truly global economy where the balance of resource power is shifting and the web of relationships is becoming more complex.

Cultural cross-national differences

David Foster (1998: 21) writes about what constitutes cross-cultural management:

> It is a shorthand term which summarises a number of different elements. First, it describes the range of organisational behaviour which exists within both countries and cultures. Second, it compares and contrasts organisational behaviour across countries and cultures. Third, it seeks to understand and improve the interaction of co-workers, clients, suppliers and partners from different countries and cultures.

The purposes of cross-cultural education and training are threefold. In the first place it is designed to encourage people to study and evaluate the components of their own culture so that they become more aware of their own hidden cultural assumptions which interfere with effective intercultural action. Second, it seeks to expand people's repertoire of culturally appropriate behaviours so that they can operate more effectively in cross-cultural encounters in the workplace. Finally, it tries to evaluate the impact of cultural factors on job performance. It can be argued that cultural traits and differences are so ingrained that it is hard for individuals even to understand they are there or that they have an influence on behaviour. There is a large body of opinion supporting the idea that different cultural traits between countries can be understood to play a part in the behaviours and ways of working prevalent among individual managers. These traits influence individual action, how relationships are formed and maintained, how products are perceived and located in markets and the success of communication.

There are a number of theories of cultural difference to guide understanding of these forces and influences. Management writer Geert Hofstede (1991) is renowned for coining the definition of culture as the collective programming of the mind. After many years of research on managers in over 70 countries, he developed a set of propositions about cultural differences based on analysis of power distance, individualism/collectivism and masculinity/femininity. Analysis of these dimensions is based on the tendencies that individual managers show towards them, and this has been built up into a categorisation of which cultures display or express strong affinity with them. In Hofstede's methodology scores were built up to suggest certain traits among different countries – for example, where a strong tendency towards collective behaviour is observed, or where a low power distance score indicates a stronger degree of cooperation between superiors and subordinates. Countries that display a strong predilection for collective action and a strong predisposition to accept power and authority will tend to work well in predominantly hierarchical, formal organisations with powerful management structures.

By combining different scores on these dimensions it is possible to group certain regional characteristics. For example, East Asian cultures display a concern for thrift and perseverance and have a high regard for social obligations and a respect for personal traditions. Further attempts at categorisation have clustered individual countries into groupings based on observed shared characteristics and affinities. For example, Ronen and Shenkar (1985) created a set of clusters based on an analysis of four key characteristics:

- the importance of work goals;
- job satisfaction;
- the impact of managerial and organisational variables;
- work roles and interpersonal orientations.

As a result they proposed eight main groupings that display shared characteristics on these dimensions.

- The Nordic states – Finland, Norway, Denmark and Sweden.
- The Germanic states – Austria, Germany and Switzerland.
- The Latin European states – France, Belgium, Portugal, Italy and Spain.
- The Latin American states – Mexico, Peru, Argentina, Chile and Venezuela.
- The Arab states – Bahrain, Abu Dhabi, Saudi Arabia, United Arab Emirates, Oman and Kuwait.
- The Near Eastern states – Turkey, Iran and Greece.
- The Anglo states – the USA, Canada, New Zealand, Australia, the UK, Ireland and South Africa.
- The Far Eastern states – Singapore, Malaysia, Hong Kong, the Philippines, Vietnam, Indonesia, Taiwan and Thailand.

Brazil, India, China and Russia are notable absentees from this list due to the date these studies were produced. Recent years have seen a flurry of research into China since the country has increasingly opened up both politically and economically. It is possible to place China in an Asian cluster, as it displays many of the characteristics of strong family ties and a tendency to collective acceptance of authority structures. However, the relationship between state control and enterprise is complex and worthy of a separate discussion later.

A problem with attempting to develop a synthesis of clusters into a model of this type is that it becomes too static and normative. It risks ignoring the dynamism of change that is so evident in societies and the world. For example, Russia was not considered at all in the earlier studies, but the fall of state Soviet power has brought great changes and opened Russia up as part of the global economy. This might suggest that it now sits with a European cluster, but that is to ignore the impact of recent history on the attitudes and perceptions of the population. Early liberalisation in Russia through the 1990s brought change but also produced a sense of chaos in the country, with loss of traditional employment, shortages and a growing crime wave. The emergence of Vladimir Putin as head of state signalled some return to stronger central control which hints of the Soviet past and has raised concern about the status of democracy and civil freedoms in Russia. However, order at the expense of some freedom seems popular in Russia – as the recent government election has indicated, with Putin and his party receiving a massive return from the electorate. The politico-economic situation in any country is a complex dynamic of cultural characteristics, history and political change which provides a defining context at any moment in time.

In economic and GDP terms this approach to clustering has been criticised for being too blunt and also for its apparent ethnocentrism, in that it represents a Western and predominantly US-based view of the world. It does give the manager some kind of indicative guide to understanding the very complex issue of how to analyse potential fit and problems when planning operations that involve different countries. For example, it is clear that negotiation will be smoother when working within the context of a cluster where there is evidence of shared characteristics. There will be a closer match between style and expectations within a cluster where similar characteristics and perceptions of outcomes pertain. The establishment of alliances or negotiations with a cluster where there are shared characteristics may be seen as simpler and thus present less risk in determining an opportunity.

Cross-cultural negotiations present much greater challenges. For example, research into American firms negotiating in Japan (Tung, 1984) found that the Japanese tended to avoid direct confrontation, took much longer to make decisions, were less flexible and were more interested in establishing a longer-term association. Failure on the part of American firms was attributed to lack of patience and a lack of understanding of the need to cultivate personal trust and a deeper relationship and the need for more mutual cooperation in business relationships. This illustrates the potential conflict between cultures: the direct approach of American managers contrasts with the Asian need for the development of trust and human relations as a precondition of a business relationship.

It is possible to analyse the cultural conditions prevalent in different countries, and indeed to group like countries together into clusters that share similar characteristics. These characteristics may provide a guide to managers about how individuals will behave in relation to work goals and indicate the cross-cultural differences which influence relationships and business behaviours such as negotiating. Cultural theorists provide detailed accounts and background, enabling managers to predict where the issues may lie in relation to working in other cultures. This suggests a need to consider whether approaches to negotiating, managing people and operations should be culturally contingent. Does a model that works in one context necessarily work in another? Some caution needs to be exercised with these models to ensure that they do not simply become a set of ethnocentric stereotypes. They are based upon the compilation of many careful research studies but, as we have seen in the case of Russia and China, it is important to take into account the dynamic nature of change and that attitudes do change over time.

The key conclusion is that national cultures do have an influence over style and behaviours that will influence how business is done. Approaches to both managing organisations and doing business need to be culturally contingent, and failure stems from not taking the time to understand that socio-cultural predispositions underpin how business is conducted.

Socio-cultural foundations and implications of current strategic thinking

The key issue to resolve is whether, in a new environment of global business activity, firms have the necessary strategic competence to compete and what questions a diverse multicultural business arena poses for current strategic thinking. It could be argued that the two main competitive pressures on businesses are those for cost reduction and local responsiveness. Responding to the pressure to reduce costs leads to attempts to standardise products and streamline production routes to achieve the greatest economies of scale. However, the pressure for local responsiveness or adaptability conflicts with this approach, requiring firms to customise product lines to suit national or regional preferences, adapt distribution channels according to local market conditions and even adapt products and marketing strategies to match local regulatory demands. These two pressures are contradictory, leading to firms compromising between these issues in strategy formulation. In formulating strategic choice, firms employ three basic strategies to compete in the international markets: multidomestic, global and transnational. These reflect the extent to which a firm must compromise between seeking cost reductions and being locally responsive.

In global conditions firms must establish that they have a competence or product that will sell into a foreign market because local competition does not have it. There is little pressure to adapt locally because domestic competition cannot provide the product, and cost pressures are low due to demand. Microsoft, for example, dominates local markets as it has secured a position as the branded office product in demand and achieved a universality which does not require local adaptation beyond basic language requirements.

A multidomestic strategy is adopted where there is strong need for local adaptation. In the automotive markets firms tend to adopt this approach, as car builds tend to reflect a number of local pressures – from design features through to safety and engine requirements. Ford has typically expanded using this approach, leading to high overhead costs in adapting and operating local plants for each market. In branded consumer markets such as packaged foods, local adaptation to suit tastes and habits predominates.

For example, a number of Western packaged foodstuffs will not translate into Asian markets as taste and habits are resistant to them except as niche products catering to a small market. The implication of this analysis is that where a product cannot be translated into a local market the business is pushed to adopt a multidomestic strategy, producing locally adapted goods for the market and selling them accordingly. Most businesses would prefer to have a global brand and production achieving economies of scale and distribution. This is inhibited if pressure for local adaptation remains strong, and in the consumer goods markets few firms have been able to achieve it.

Theodore Levitt (1983) predicted the rise of global markets and the end of regional differences and tastes; the current evidence does not support this. Even global brands such as McDonalds and Coke make allowances for local adaptation. The McDonalds menu is modified in different countries to suit local consumer preferences, and while Coke is marketed as a global brand in terms of image, the recipe is tailored to different regional tastes. Proctor and Gamble initially found it difficult to break into the Japanese market as its product range did not match consumer preference or expectations. The company learned to tailor its product lines more to the local tastes and began to have success. Proctor and Gamble has a wide range of detergent and laundry products under the same brand names, but the actual nature of the product is subtly adapted for local preferences.

The nature of and approaches to advertising may be similarly influenced. In emerging and developing economies firms are discovering that direct TV advertising that was successful in the 1960s in the West is working in these markets, whereas it would generate consumer resistance now in the West. Media in these countries are not as developed or mature. Evidently this will change over time.

Early attempts by US companies to operate in China were frustrated because the direct-selling approach on which the US business had been built was outlawed by state regulation.

A global strategy can be adopted where the pressures on costs are high, particularly in production and research and development, and profitability stems from containing costs in these areas, but the pressure for local customisation is relatively low. This is more typical of industrial goods markets where firms build and sell products rather than direct consumer goods. Typically markets that do not involve consumer goods are less driven by local tastes, as they are not subject to fashion or tastes and preferences that may be informed by local habit or custom. Production costs are contained by locating in small numbers of sites where costs of production are favourable due to availability of labour, plant, energy and supplies. A global player will seek to market standardised products and avoid customisation, operating through centralised production and chains of supply. Here trade barriers and product standards will have greater influence.

A transnational strategy occurs where firms have to attempt to meet the major conflicting demands of high cost pressures and high demand for local responsiveness. Firms seek to achieve differentiation through adaptation of products or services while pursuing lower costs. This is an extremely difficult state to achieve and maintain. An example is the case of Caterpillar, which met increased global competition from the Japanese company Komatsu by developing plants in major market centres while ruthlessly streamlining and standardising many of the components of its core products. In this way the business was able to re-engineer its costs significantly while becoming customer facing in local markets due to relocations. Local plants carried out assemblies with a small number of locally tailored features. This enabled the company to win back significant market share by the end of the 1990s.

Table 3.1 summarises the three main strategies available to firms in meeting the global challenge. The table indicates that a transnational strategic approach offers the best in terms of advantages; the only disadvantage is that it is hard to organise and consequently suggests a greater degree of managerial challenge. Bartlett and Ghoshal (1989) have presented the case for transnational strategies as the only real response to increasing global pressures. While it is evident that this is a difficult strategy to pursue and would not fit many businesses in terms of their available resources, it is worth exploring further in the context of the rapid increase

Table 3.1   Global challenge: three main strategies

Strategy	Advantages	Disadvantages
Global	Develop experience-curve effects Develop location economies	Lack of local responsiveness
Multidomestic	Customise product offerings and marketing in accordance with local responsiveness	Inability to realise location economies Failure to develop experience-curve effects Failure to transfer distinctive competencies to foreign markets
Transnational	Develop experience-curve effects Develop location economies Customise product offerings and marketing in accordance with local responsiveness Reap benefits of global learning	Difficult to implement due to organisational problems

in global competitive pressure over the last ten years. A firm is able to pursue the benefits of local responsiveness through better understanding and exploitation of the market, leading to more effective product placement. In essence, firms must exploit experience-based economies and location economies, they must transfer core competencies within the firm and they must do all this while paying attention to pressures for local responsiveness. In this kind of firm, core competencies do not only reside in the home location – they may stem from any location as divisions or subsidiaries in different countries become increasingly more expert in what does and does not work and the organisation is able to share and exploit that knowledge. The key issue distinguishing a firm that can be described as transnational is the extent to which there is knowledge development, learning and sharing between different locations in the business. The flow of skills, insights, ideas and product knowledge is more than one way, from company to outlets, and becomes multidirectional. This is referred to as global learning (that is, a willingness and ability to exploit locally derived knowledge and transfer it through the firm, such that it can be developed elsewhere or used in product, supply-chain and market development), and is the key strategic aspect to this approach.

There is no doubt that to organise a transnational approach does present great managerial challenges. To operate effectively where there is global scope for tailoring while maintaining a corporate sense of product costs and controls requires significant coordination. If the controls are not effective the firm will simply splinter into many units of activity, the creative advantage of locally derived experience will be stifled and the business will not thrive. Moreover, local competition will always have an advantage if a global firm cannot respond effectively and rapidly in shaping a market because it is bogged down in corporate decision-making.

Samuel Palmisano, chair and CEO of IBM, rehearsed this issue in an influential piece published in *Foreign Affairs* in 2006. Reflecting on the current status of the multinational corporation in the context of the new global economic challenges, he suggests that the MNC is taking on a new form and moving to being 'global' rather than 'multinational'.[1] He outlines the need for change that is structural, operational and cultural in response to the imperatives of globalisation and technology. The modern global firm will transform from the multinational, with its imprint of a national business working in other markets, to a globally integrated enterprise where the firm transcends national boundaries and operates as a network moving high-value skills, knowledge, service and products to wherever they are needed using integrated supply chains. IBM as a business is moving towards this model, where everything is connected and the organisation is a fully networked business. Hans Ulrich Maerki (2007) describes it as an open networked business integrated into the fabric of a networked economy, with the following key features:

- makes informed choices within a global competitive market;
- secures value via specialisation in a network of collaborative partners;
- taps into a universe of modular services;
- operates seamlessly across boundaries via global values, skills and processes;
- embraces open collaboration and shared intellectual property, policies and practices;
- leverages the power of global assets.

The business now locates key divisions around the globe where they achieve the best fit to economic drivers, and has many different nationalities as leaders. The current development of IBM as both a business and an organisation seems to be embracing the real meaning of a transnational strategy. There is a genuine emphasis on a global (as opposed to a multinational) philosophy, alongside networked and integrated operations and a management structure with a desire for knowledge leverage and learning across the whole world. This is coupled to investment in emerging markets and a series of alliances in those markets. A transnational approach with a globally integrated enterprise as the organisational response forms a template for how to respond to the twenty-first-century globalisation challenge.

Inherent capabilities within the socio-technical dimension of international management

International business and global trade are not impersonal, abstract issues. They are personal, and involve the interaction of cultures, peoples and styles. The success of any global strategy will depend on the extent to which people can interact successfully and increasingly work in effective global teams. The question here is: does the business have the necessary capabilities to manage successfully in a more diverse and complex business environment? The challenges facing the global manager in this environment are summarised as:

- integrating large international organisations;
- understanding the meaning of performance and accountability in a globally integrated system of product flows;
- building and managing a worldwide logistics capability;

- developing country-specific corporate strategies that take into account the political and economic imperatives;

- forming and benefiting from collaborative arrangements around the world;

- balancing the pressures for global integration and local demands.

Research into cultural differences has tended to emphasise the distance between cultures. To a large extent this has become a narrative of stereotypes. Any attempt to classify national cultures is going to run into difficulties in terms of how these differences are described, what tools of measurement are employed and the static nature of taking a snapshot in time and history. Putting aside the problems of classification, it is recognised that national cultural differences can be deeply embedded, leading to contrasts in style and behaviour that affect how managers act and respond to situations. For example, Chung (1991) argues that the psychology of thinking styles explains differences in business cultures. He argues that Europeans are taught to think in a linear way, whereas Asians learn to see things as a whole. Europeans value rational logic, while Asians think intuitively. For example, Asian managers will tend to look to their personal networks to glean subjective qualitative data. These managers will involve themselves personally much more, and more deeply, in the minutiae of their organisations to obtain data than would an Occidental manager, who may rely more on secondary data sources and mathematical analyses (Kidd, 2001).

The management of cross-cultural teams or operations in other cultures poses a number of challenges. The universal application of management theories and regimes does not always produce the desired results: there are many examples of companies attempting to manage and impose regimes that are norms in the West but lead to failure in other contexts. For example, Abdullah and Singh (1992) described how attempts to impose an American approach to the management and motivation of the domestic workforce in a Malaysian subsidiary produced conflicts and disputes. The managers most likely to motivate the staff were those who could understand the local cultural requirement for good relations and respect. When DaimlerChrysler opened operations in Thailand it attempted to use the models that were common in its German plants. These contrasted so much with expected norms of behaviour that rapid turnover of staff occurred and there were a number of labour disputes. Huo and Steers (1993) describe how even the technical design of incentive systems needs take account of the domestic culture, arguing that competitive financial bonus arrangements do not work as well in some Asian societies where harmonious social relations and cooperation prevail as a cultural norm.

Basic management systems and behavioural approaches need to be culture-contingent in the same way that product strategies need to reflect the habits and tastes of the local market. Increasingly MNEs are placing local managers in charge rather than importing expertise from the home base, and working on the development of global teams who can recognise each other's strengths and knowledge and draw all aspects into building global strategies. Major corporations like IBM now have many European and Asian nationals running key divisions as part of the firm's emergence as a global integrated enterprise. David Lennard (2006), writing in the *Asia Times*, noted that for foreign firms in China one of the most significant recent developments is the handover from expatriate to local managers who are much better equipped to operate in the emerging environment. He predicts this as a growing trend for foreign firms in China, as those which do not utilise local managers will not be able to succeed, their reputations will suffer and they will not be able to attract the best talent.

Overseeing cultural diversity

With respect to global strategies, firms require managers who can work together across cultural barriers and who recognise that there will be differences. An ethnocentric view that there is one best model or way of doing things will not help to develop and implement suitable transnational strategies. Trust is fundamental for people who have to accomplish important tasks together, but how managers build trust is individually and culturally determined. How managers perceive cultural diversity and use it for competitive advantage is arguably the greatest challenge faced by many corporate boards. In *The Cultural Advantage: A New Model for Succeeding with Global Teams*, Huijser (2006) proposes a model of freedom which enables teams and individuals to develop to their strengths by using different cultural viewpoints to build decision-making which respects each other's orientation. Based on over 20 years' experience of working in Asia and Europe, Huijser recognises that culture could be seen as a constraint that can be used as an advantage.

In business we have the choice either to deny the importance of cultural differences and take whatever it costs to sustain this conviction, or to use the differences as potential energy that becomes available if we can put our norms in a cultural perspective. Our culture is our advantage. Although many international businesses have become increasingly competent in technology, production and the management of capital assets, few have mastered the complexities of managing cultural assets. Adding such cultural assets (to ours) is one of the greatest challenges faced by many firms in the twenty-first century. One of the key reasons for global business failure is the poor dynamics of intercultural experience. These dynamics include differences in cultural perceptions, in values and practices that influence understanding, in attitudinal satisfaction with living in a foreign culture, in relationship development and in the accomplishment of goals. Intercultural consultant Gary Wederspahn (2000) argues that employees who have cross-border responsibilities and/or cross-cultural relationships need to be prepared to handle the inevitable intercultural tasks and challenges involved. The assertion here is that global businesses in the future will be concerned with how to leverage the best of each culture and how cultural assets can be used creatively to influence future strategic direction in international competition. This implies developing cultural assets across different market boundaries and managing international operations that reflect global as opposed to international strategies.

Key chapter messages

- Increasing migration and business opportunities have produced broader levels of interaction across cultures and business domains.

- All the emerging markets in the BRIC nations display one similar characteristic: they all have large and rapid growth rates. The growth has been initiated and is typically dominated by development in the large metropolitan areas where increasing middle-class populations are driving economic demand and change through increased consumer spending on a range of domestic goods.

■ The Eastern economies are beginning to take a large and direct stake in the markets and businesses of the West. This major socio-economic shift is leading to an increasing and inexorable interdependence between business managers and owners from different cultures.

■ There is a large body of opinion that supports the idea that different cultural traits between countries can be understood to play a part in the behaviours and ways of working prevalent among individual managers.

■ Countries that display a strong predilection for collective action and a strong predisposition to accept power and authority will tend towards working well in predominantly hierarchical, formal organisations with powerful management structures.

■ The politico-economic situation in any country is a complex dynamic of cultural characteristics, history and political change which provides a defining context at any moment in time.

■ The two main competitive pressures on businesses are the pressure for cost reduction and the pressure for local responsiveness. Responding to the pressure to reduce costs leads to attempts to standardise products and streamline production routes to achieve the greatest economies of scale.

■ In formulating strategic choice, firms employ three basic strategies to compete in international markets: multidomestic, global and transnational. These reflect the extent to which a firm must compromise between seeking cost reductions and being locally responsive.

- The management of cross-cultural teams or operations in other cultures poses a number of challenges. The universal application of management theories and regimes does not always produce the desired results.

- In business we have the choice either to deny the importance of cultural differences and take whatever it costs to sustain this conviction, or to use the differences as potential energy that becomes available if we can put our norms in a cultural perspective.

Note

1. Writers on strategy occasionally use the terms 'international' and 'multinational' (firms) interchangeably.

4

The forces that shape strategic effectiveness in global markets

Determining global, national and strategic aspirations

Since the days of Adam Smith, firms have grappled with the challenge of exploiting their competitive advantage to increase their markets and profits. The model for most of the twentieth century was of a large integrated firm that managed its own assets, in part protected by the nation-state. According to Michael Porter (1990), competitive advantage arises from the value a firm is able to create for its buyers, whether that value is based on lower costs or on unique benefits (differentiation) that offset a price for the product or service provided. In 1985 Porter was appointed to President Reagan's Commission on Industrial Competitiveness.[1] The commission was made up of senior industrialists, government officials and academics, none of whom could agree on a definition of competitiveness. To many business leaders it generally meant the ability to compete in world markets; to many government officials it meant a favourable balance of trade. Although some academics will argue the point, it could be said that prior to Porter's appointment there was no generally accepted theory to explain competitiveness. That changed in 1990 when

Porter published *The Competitive Advantage of Nations*, bringing a new theoretical perspective to bear on the impact of location on the prosperity of nations or states. Porter observed:

> I began with a microeconomic point of view – individual firms and industries – which complemented the more top-down, macroeconomic perspective that had long predominated. In particular, I focused on the effect of clusters – geographic concentrations of interconnected companies, specialized suppliers, service providers, and firms in related industries – on innovation and success.

One of the key findings from Porter's work was that nations succeed in particular industries because their home environment is the most forward-looking, dynamic and challenging, contradicting many of the conventionally held beliefs about international competitiveness, which focused on labour costs, interest rates, exchange rates, economies of scale and supranational globalisation (Figure 4.1).

It could be argued that the ability to be forward-looking and dynamic is inherent in a nation's ability to maintain an aspirational position relative to the market. To some extent this is influenced by the decisions taken by governments and business leaders. Government attention to managing resource flows effectively (in the EU for example) has seen the growth of research organisations able to model the resource economy and support policy formulation by life-cycle thinking. The result of this shift in thinking is evident in the growing economic stature of the BRIC nations: their increasing dominance is in many respects a direct consequence of ambitious national macroeconomic policies and business decisions taken in the last decade to improve economic conditions and resource utilisation. To emphasise

Figure 4.1   Attributes of competitiveness

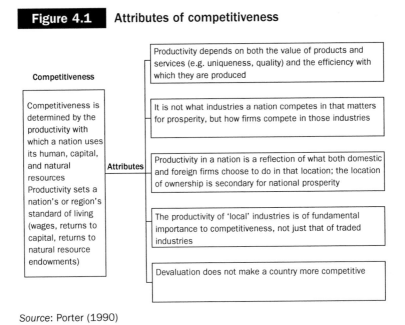

Competitiveness

Competitiveness is determined by the productivity with which a nation uses its human, capital, and natural resources
Productivity sets a nation's or region's standard of living (wages, returns to capital, returns to natural resource endowments)

Attributes

Productivity depends on both the value of products and services (e.g. uniqueness, quality) and the efficiency with which they are produced

It is not what industries a nation competes in that matters for prosperity, but how firms compete in those industries

Productivity in a nation is a reflection of what both domestic and foreign firms choose to do in that location; the location of ownership is secondary for national prosperity

The productivity of 'local' industries is of fundamental importance to competitiveness, not just that of traded industries

Devaluation does not make a country more competitive

Source: Porter (1990)

this point, in the mid-1990s Brazil made a policy shift to open up to the global economy. As a result of structural reform and trade liberalisation, the economy recovered on an export-led[2] growth path which could see Brazil as one of the top five economies in the world by 2050 (Table 4.1).[3]

The case for Brazil's emerging industry (software and technology)

Fifteen years ago the research arm of Brazil's Ministry of Science and Technology gathered a community of academics, industrialists, entrepreneurs and government policy-makers. The goal was to define a strategic programme that would eventually replace Brazil's existing information technology policy. At that time a strict policy regulated the internal market, protecting the local information technology industry. Today, much of Brazil's

| Table 4.1 | Top ten in GNP, 2005 versus 2050 |

2005			2050		
Rank	Country	GNP (US$ billion)	Rank	Country	GNP (US$ billion)
1	USA	11,351	1	China	44,453
2	Japan	4,366	2	USA	35,165
3	Germany	1,966	3	India	27,803
4	UK	1,647	4	Japan	6,673
5	China	1,529	5	Brazil	6,074
6	France	1,445	6	Russia	5,870
7	Italy	1,212	7	UK	3,782
8	Canada	728	8	Germany	3,603
9	Spain	665	9	France	3,148
10	Mexico	642	10	Italy	2,061

Source: Goldman Sachs (2003)

software industry is concentrated in Rio de Janeiro and São Paulo, but there are important emerging centres in Santa Catarina and Rio Grande do Sul; in Santa Catarina there are 600 software and related enterprises with total revenues of US$250 million and employing 7,000 people. Small firms dominate in number, but a few foreign multinationals have come to take the leadership in a very fragmented market. For example, in network systems the American Novell do Brazil holds 80 per cent of the market; smaller firms, which had some market presence, have been forced to seek niche markets, become distributors of foreign programs or develop custom applications for popular foreign programs.

Although Brazil is the world's seventh-largest software producer, only a fraction of the industry's revenues are earned through exports. Like China, the Brazilian software industry has benefited from its hardware industry, in that the need of domestic manufacturers for embedded software gives advantages to domestic software producers. This point leads some analysts to believe that one strategy for growth would be to focus on software for the domestic sector.[4] Although China and India are more advanced in software capability, Brazil is attempting to increase its capabilities and market presence. Since the new millennium Brazil has become a favoured target for many multinational firms as a key revenue source because of the country's economic growth, stability and consumer preference for US technology. According to a KPMG study, Brazil's financial sector – Latin America's largest and most sophisticated – continues to expand its software use. Recent spending on third-party software grew 70 per cent and on internally developed software 46 per cent, a trend expected to continue (KPMG, 2005: 11–29). A key goal of the Brazilian government is to build on its performance and create a thriving software market to increase its software exports to US$1.5 billion by 2007, thereby approaching the level of revenue generated by China and India.

The Brazilian ICT industry's positive performance has not been limited to the financial domain. Estimates indicate that the number of jobs grew threefold between 1996 and 2001, reaching over 200,000. By the end of this period software and service companies employed nearly 65 per cent of ICT workers; the same proportion of international employers placed their jobs in locally owned companies. In 2000 the number of ICT workers with a PhD exceeded 2,000, with most degrees held in software-related fields (Duarte and Branco, 2001). As Brazil's ICT market has grown, a number of foreign software and information services firms have set up local subsidiaries for localisation and various services, including Microsoft, SAP, Novell, Progress Software, Andersen Consulting and EDS. Motorola recently set up a centre to develop embedded software for cellular phones.

Former national macroeconomic policies that were sometimes dissociated from public efforts to promote economic growth have hindered Brazil's software industry growth. Previously the country had serious problems with exponentially increasing inflation, but the introduction of a new national currency nearly ten years ago helped solve these. The high value of the local currency in relation to the American dollar for most of the past decade, combined with continuing high interest rates diverting investment from production and export, contributed to reducing the local industry's external competitiveness. More recently the Brazilian software industry has become more competitive, and the amount of activity in the sector shows the strength of Brazil's ICT market: ICT transactions tripled in the first half of 2005; sales of management software such as ERP and CRM have doubled over the past two years; e-commerce continues to increase; the country has emerged as Latin America's most attractive outsourcing market; and Brazil's wireless market is growing faster than that in the USA, and it may emerge as one of the world's most important wireless security technology markets. Lastly, the federal government is a large and sophisticated software user – its e-government initiatives, such as electronic voting and the e-filing of 95 per cent of personal income taxes and 100 per cent of corporate taxes, have bolstered Brazil's e-reputation.

Brazil has a number of wealthy consumers and a supply of low-cost talent in some key sectors. Growth rates have reached 3.6 per cent, according to the World Bank (2007). Political stability still remains a problem. Further progress will also depend on the global economy and the strength of the US economy, as well as the policy on interest rates and currency fluctuations. The challenges facing the Brazilian software industry are enormous, despite the industry's strengths (Table 4.2). Given Brazil's domestic commitments it is highly unlikely that its ICT industry will make any significant strides in exports, at least in the short term. To start exporting

Table 4.2   A view of Brazil's current capability

PEST	High-level overview of strengths
Political environment	Stronger political affiliations with Western governments Strong political support for domestic markets Increased regulatory reforms Increased political support for tax breaks
Economic environment	Competitive labour-cost model Increasing growth rate in software sector Improved export position Improved infrastructure
Societal environment	Increased employability in software markets Increased support for education Increased support for entrepreneurship
Technological environment	Strong ties with Western technology companies Improving research and development culture Increasing number of science graduates (PhDs) Adaptive to new technologies and innovation

software effectively and still meet local market demands, it is fundamental for the country to be capable of developing and producing internally complete solutions in which hardware, software and services are intertwined. This would appear possible only if Brazil controls the production cycle of electronic components. To get round this issue the Ministry of Development, Industry and Commerce is currently engaging with external partners to agree technology contracts and innovation partnerships (Duarte, 2002).

The case for China's emerging industry

A wide range of business leaders, politicians, economic analysts and technological optimists promote the advantages of economic growth that comes from sustainable developments in national strategies. In contrast to Brazil, business and government leaders in China have sought to use

China's openness to foreign investment to acquire technology and management expertise and use competition from foreign firms operating in China to prepare Chinese companies to compete in the global economy. Three objectives are prominent: opening new markets for Chinese goods and labour; building national champions, brands and distribution networks; and acquiring advanced technology.

China's development strategy has emphasised exports to major developed country markets such as the USA, Japan and Western Europe. Exports to these markets have grown rapidly, but are beginning to stimulate protectionist reactions. China has sought to diversify and develop new export markets, paying particular attention to developing countries in Asia, Latin America and Africa.

In terms of building national champions, brands and distribution networks, Chinese exports are booming, but about 60 per cent are produced by foreign-funded enterprises based in China. The percentage is even higher in high-technology sectors such as industrial machinery (79 per cent), computers (92 per cent) and electronics and telecommunications (74 per cent). Many Chinese companies are locked into low-value-added niches in global supply chains with limited opportunity to innovate or earn large profits. Chinese policy-makers want to build national companies that can compete internationally. This was one motive behind the 'grasp the big, let go of the small' approach to privatising state-owned enterprises. Chinese companies such as Haier, TCL-Thompson and Lenovo have all recently pursued acquisitions of foreign businesses in order to obtain internationally recognised brands and access to established distribution networks.

Haier, China's leading home-appliance manufacturer, has faced increasingly tough competition in the domestic market, which accounts for 80 per cent of its sales. Haier has had zero profit growth for the last three years, which led executives to expand further into the US market. Weaknesses in design skills and distribution and service networks limited Haier's success and prompted the company to make a $1.28 billion bid in 2005 to buy Maytag. Haier sought Maytag's brand name and sales network, but ultimately was outbid by Whirlpool. Chinese computer maker Lenovo purchased IBM's personal computer business in December 2004 for $1.75 billion. The acquisition was motivated by increasing competition and falling profits in the domestic market, and by Lenovo's desire to have an internationally recognised brand name that would allow it to compete effectively at the global level.

Regarding acquiring advanced technology, Chinese firms seek to use acquisitions or joint ventures to obtain technology necessary to improve their competitive ability. Joint ventures with foreign firms investing in China have been a primary means of acquiring technology in the past, but China's WTO commitments now allow foreign firms to establish wholly owned subsidiaries (thus avoiding the need to share technology with Chinese partners). This provides increased incentives for Chinese firms to pursue technology by acquiring foreign companies. For example, Huawei, a major Chinese telecommunications manufacturer, has expressed interest in purchasing the British firm Marconi. Shanghai Automotive Industry Corporation (SAIC), a leading Chinese auto manufacturer, purchased Korean automaker SsangYong Motors for $500 million in October 2004. Access to the Korean firm's technology and research and development capability was an important motive for the deal (Saunders, 2006).

Determining global strategic forces and behaviour

In their book *Military Misfortunes: The Anatomy of Failure in War*, distinguished military historians Eliot Cohen and

John Gooch (1990) astutely observe that the militaries of modern democracies fail because they do not anticipate changes on the battlefield (*markets*), learn to fight in new environments (*business*) or adapt to the changing nature of war (*rules of engagement*). It is sometimes difficult for a successful firm to look beyond the horizon and see the inevitable changes that must occur in structure and strategy to maintain a competitive advantage in the marketplace. GE managed to maintain a dominant position in its chosen markets for over two decades; according to Welch (2005: 171), 'if they're headed in the right direction and are broad enough, strategies don't really need to change all that often, especially if they are supplemented with fresh initiatives'. To that end, over the years GE launched four programmes to bolster its strategy: globalisation, service add-ons, Six Sigma and e-business. Welch's line of argument was very simple – commoditisation is wicked and people are everything. Virtually every resource allocation decision made in GE was based on those beliefs. Although individuals may have different interpretations of Welch's philosophy and ideas when analysing the strategic forces and behaviour that shape many of today's worldwide businesses decisions, two critical forces are prominent: 'market' and 'political' influences.

Market influences

Since the publication of Porter's (1980) work on competitive strategy, the argument that firms must select between generic strategies has been frequently debated and challenged by both academics and managers alike. Although revolutionary in its day, the model developed by Porter is now too simplistic. The competitive environment and the market forces inherent within it have become more hostile. Growing competition from the BRIC nations and the globalisation of markets have combined to make business increasingly complex. Instability in many markets due to political, economic and social upheaval, coupled with pace of change and shorter product life cycles, has increased uncertainty and dynamism in all but a few specialist markets. Niches that were once protected by brand or other entry barriers are being penetrated. No firm seems to be immune from price competition, and being customer-focused and delivering excellent value are order-qualifying rather than order-winning capabilities.

Markets today have moved beyond segmentation. Consumer forces have increased the pace to such an extent that some firms have given up on marketing altogether and turned to alternative forms of product advertising. A growing number of firms now meet the needs of segments-of-one in which the seller makes available a flexible market offering. One example of this is the trend towards consumer-generated advertising that allows users to personalise the content before sending it on. Business leaders such as Jeff Bezos, CEO and chairman of Amazon.com, argue that firms must establish a distinct and valued core in the marketplace. Smart firms seek to own a position in their target customers' minds. Bezos's particular genius was realising that logistics, warehousing and incredibly powerful software that would help him with shipping were what was going to set Amazon apart from the competition. Amazon customers can search for the book title they want and order online. Tens of thousands of titles are discounted by between 10 and 40 per cent, so the customer is getting considerable value for money too. Amazon customers can signal their interest in, say, a particular author and they will be notified by e-mail of new books of interest. This new online business model deals direct with customers and bypasses the traditional (place-based) bookstore. It also establishes a new form of cybercompetitor which is competing along a different dimension – breadth of titles – that is costly to replicate in the existing physical model. Wholesaler and retailer margins get shared out between the customers, in the form of lower prices, and Amazon.com in profits.

Coping with such emerging changes in technology, demographics, economics and distribution management requires a different approach to decision-making and thinking. Too many firms are inside-out thinkers, not outside-in thinkers. They are product-oriented, not market-oriented. Many technology firms spend millions on research and development without ever consulting their end users. In the 1990s General Motors designed cars that it thought consumers should have. It thought the marketing job was to sell cars, not to design them.[5] Outside-in firms such as Sony, Apple and Microsoft take their clues from the marketplace. They take consumer advice, spot unmet needs and translate them into business opportunities (Apple's sixth-generation iPod is expected to sport a unique 3.5-inch touch-screen display geared towards video playback). Outside-in firms like Apple have defined target groups and developed a value-added system that is superior to that of competitors serving the same market.

Bringing the customer directly into the design process can dramatically change the ability to develop fast market responses to customer needs. Levi's, for example, is using technology at the point of purchase to obtain information on customer size requirements for jeans (Summers, 1996). It uses this information to custom-manufacture bespoke jeans for the individual lady customer and deliver these at a 40 per cent price premium. This information asset is then bar-coded into the jeans and the customer can reorder to suit her size at any time. Understanding and responding to the information exchanged at the point of consumption enhance both customer loyalty and differentiation (price premium).

Political influences

For better or worse, governments have a great influence on the way firms conduct business and the way markets are regulated, controlled and managed. In the book *Marketing Places* Kotler et al. (1999) describe the theory and practices used by national governments and business groups to build their economy by attracting needed resources, such as research and development assets. An important trend regarding global competitiveness is the internationalisation of research and development and the inherent government forces which come into play. Today, the sources of competitive advantage of multinational enterprises do not lie in their home countries 'alone', but are spread over a number of locations and different countries.

For example, the Republic of Ireland (RoI) has attracted hundreds of foreign companies and millions of euros in investment. In order to manage its future economic aspirations, the Irish government created a number of separate ministries. Their purpose is to oversee future expansion of the economy and smooth the pathway for technical and business innovation. Twenty years ago Ireland was a technology follower; today the RoI is a leader in many areas of technology such as semiconductors, software and data communications. In 2001 the Irish government established a new organisation called Science Foundation Ireland (SFI) to develop the RoI as a centre for research and development excellence in strategic areas relevant to economic development. Initial emphasis is on biotechnology and ICT, and the overall governance of SFI will ensure industrial input into its priority-setting processes. It is expected that universities will be the major research performers funded by SFI.

The economist Joseph Stigler (1968: 67) defined an entry barrier as: 'A cost of producing (at some or every rate of output) which must be borne by a firm which seeks to enter an industry but is not borne by firms already in the industry.' One of the major barriers to entry is spending on research and development. Heavy spending on R&D can act as a strong deterrent to potential entrants to any industry. Clearly much R&D spending goes on developing new products, but there are also important spill-over effects which allow firms to improve their production processes and reduce unit costs. This makes the existing firms more competitive in the market and gives them a structural advantage over potential rival firms. Within the OECD, support for innovation is relatively high (Figure 4.2). One measure of innovation efficiency is the ability of firms to translate innovation inputs into innovation outputs. The ratio between inputs (education, investment in innovation, etc.) and outputs (firm turnover coming from new products, employment in high-tech sectors, patents, etc.) provides a measure of this relationship for national innovation systems.

Figure 4.2 **Estimated R&D expenditure, USA versus OECD, 1990–2003**

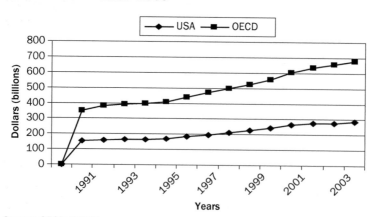

Source: OECD (2006)

Although the growth in innovation and entrepreneurship within the EU has brought many benefits to member countries, it has also created many challenges. In high-tech products, Europe's impressive inventive performance has not translated into overall market success. While registering a high proportion of world patents, the EU's trade balance in high-technology products in real terms is poor in comparison to a decade ago. Extrapolated figures for 2003 show the US high-technology industry accounting for more than 40 per cent of global value added, the EU for about 18 per cent and Japan for about 12 per cent. Although there are conflicting opinions, the medium-technology markets have suffered the most in that the R&D funds associated with this sector have been diverted into fighting off rival products from low-cost producers such as Taiwan, South Korea and China. Rapid acceleration of inward investment into low-cost producing countries such as China has been responsible for the diversion of domestic funding into high-technology sectors such as defence. The US aerospace industry has long maintained a leading if not dominant position in the global marketplace. In recent years, however, the aerospace industry's manufacturing share has fallen more than that of any other US industry. The US share of global aerospace production is estimated to have fallen to about 35 per cent in 2003. At its highest level in 1985, US aerospace accounted for 57 per cent of global production.

Determining global success factors within a firm

A firm's competitiveness and its associated strengths and weaknesses tend to evolve slowly and cannot be adequately described by looking at just a few key indicators, such as return on investment. In the construction of any business

Figure 4.3   Three Cs strategic triangle

Corporation

Strategic triangle

Competition

Customer

strategy, three entities must be taken into consideration: the *corporation* (or firm) itself, the *customer* and the *competition*, collectively know as the strategic triangle (Ohmae, 1982). Seen in the context of the strategic triangle (Figure 4.3), the role of the CEO is to achieve superior performance relative to the competition. At the same time, the CEO must be sure that the underlying strategy accurately matches the strengths of the firm within the needs of a clearly defined market. Positive matching of customer needs and the firm's marketing objectives is required for a lasting good relationship; without it, the firm's long-term viability is at stake.

The corporation (or firm)

In formulating business strategy the corporation (or firm) is in many respects wedded to its history, culture and reputation. One of the most influential books in the last 25 years, *In Search of Excellence* by Peters and Waterman (1982), considered a number of firms believed to be innovative and strategically excellent.[6] In their prescriptions on excellence, the authors identified a number of key factors that enhance innovation and a firm's competitive position. Although by no means exhaustive, these included:

- focusing on satisfying customer needs;
- building a profitable, competitive supply chain;
- building systems for innovation;
- providing leadership and a strong commitment of resources.

A dilemma for many CEOs is deciding where to invest their limited resources. The key here is for CEOs to make choices about what businesses and parts of the supply chain can be built into competitively strong platforms for future innovation (capability) and markets. In this respect firms must assess possible futures and risks: according to Sir John Harvey Jones (2005), time and advance warnings are the key things enabling a CEO to take advantage of the capability to change and react far faster than large competitors. No longer has any business man or woman an excuse for not spending ten minutes every morning or evening checking the current state of their business.

> That is when the development of a trend can be spotted – remember, you cannot do anything about numbers, you can only do things about trends. And because speed is a key competitive area, the quicker you pick up the trend, the faster you gain the advantage. The absolute key factor of all is speed. (Ibid.)

Here scenarios and risk assessments demonstrate long-term resource constraints, trade-offs and opportunities that may result from alternative futures. The key is often the quality of the risk assessments made and true openness to learning from past performance. Too often managers see the risks from customers, competitors, technology and supply being talked up or down to justify a previously determined course rather than subjected to objective scrutiny. Similarly, it is crucial to understand the true reasons for past success and failure – since they rapidly enter the corporate mythology for judging future action.

For example, after decades of continual success, Coca-Cola found itself facing a series of problems as it entered the new millennium.[7] During the 1970s and 1980s the firm expanded its global reach into almost 200 countries. At that time the company began to centralise control and encourage consolidation among all bottling partners. In the 1990s, however, the world began to change. Many national and local leaders began seeking sovereignty over their political, economic and cultural futures. As a result, the very forces that were making the world more connected and homogeneous were also triggering a powerful desire for local autonomy and the preservation of unique cultural identity. In essence the world was demanding more agility, responsiveness and sincerity from MNEs, while Coca-Cola was centralising decision-making, standardising operating practices and insulating itself from this changing environment. Coca-Cola was going global when it should have been going local (Daft, 2000).

The customer

To reinforce our understanding of customer needs we are predictably urged to convert insights into choices about how the firm can deliver value and consider redesigning the organisation along customer segment lines, communicating the new focus internally via performance measures and building in customer feedback mechanisms. According to Doug Daft (ibid.):

> we must remember we do not do business in markets; we do business in societies... In our future, we'll succeed because we will also understand and appeal to local differences. The 21st century demands nothing less.

Assuming one agrees with this statement, the implications for how firms develop market and marketing strategies become paramount to future revenues and profits. For example, theoretically it is possible to maintain a uniform product strategy, pricing strategy, distribution strategy and promotional strategy on a global scale. Practically, more or less extensive adjustments in the marketing mix have to be taken into consideration when a company strives to achieve globalism in its business activities. When Saatchi and Saatchi, the UK advertising firm, decided to branch out into North America by acquiring the Bates advertising agency, it decided to build a global service offering for MNEs by expanding its core advertising business to include a communications and public relations division and a consulting division. The objective of these efforts was to become a global service provider using a recognised brand name. Unfortunately, the Saatchi organisation lacked the requisite skills for integrating its approach into local markets. Management failed to grasp that advertising, communication and consulting have to be geared towards local clients and a global vanilla-based approach will not succeed. As a result, the firm's expansion into the US market and its globalisation efforts proved to be major failures.

Management always, and understandably, considers its product or service to be important. If it did not, it could not do a good job. Nonetheless, to the customer, no product or service, and certainly no firm, is of much importance.

Emergent thinking on *open business models* indicates a move towards individual customer value systems. The customer only wants what the product or service will do for him tomorrow. All he is interested in are his own values, his own wants and his own reality. For this reason alone, any serious attempt to state what 'our' business is must start with the customer, his realities, situation, behaviour, expectations and values. In essence, to survive in the long term firms have to be adaptive and display market attributes of tailoring, difference, concentration, independence, flexibility and separation.

The competition

Porter's (1998) five forces model states that the rules of competition for any industry – whether domestic or international, producing product or service – are embodied in the entry of new competitors; the threat of substitutes; the bargaining power of buyers; the bargaining power of suppliers; and the rivalry among existing competitors. Although not necessarily conventional wisdom from an economic perspective, there is a need to base all analysis of competition in a market context, which in turn entails defining the relevant economic product markets before proceeding to analyse the extent of competition within that market and subsequently within the industry.

The first step is the definition of the market, or markets. Market definition is not an end in itself, but a tool used to identify the boundaries within which competition takes place. As such, it needs to be carried out on a case-by-case basis. Market definitions can and do change over time as new opportunities for demand- and supply-side substitution arise. Market definition also has indirect benefits in that it helps uncover and prioritise other pieces of economic evidence, such as who a firm's competitors are and the form of any barriers to market entry.

Take the case of Proctor and Gamble (P&G). With annual sales of $68 billion and a capitalisation of $200 billion, P&G has operations in 80 countries around the world employing around 140,000 people. In carrying out its operations P&G employs a business model that combines high national responsiveness with high economic integration. For P&G this has not always been the case. In 2000 the firm's share price began to plummet, losing more than half its value between January and May. After careful analysis of the situation, P&G realised its poor performance was because it was not developing enough 'new brands', and the only way to develop new brands was to be more open. The firm instigated a restructuring initiative, called Connect and Develop; it grouped its 200-plus brands into five major business units, adopting open innovation and an open business model. Each business is coordinated globally from different locations around the world. These business units are 'global' units in a highly decentralised approach, with strategies being developed and implemented locally and regionally. In particular the units are responsible for spreading product innovations across the company's product categories and geographic markets. In addition to units formed along product lines, P&G also has market development organisations, which are geographically organised. P&G uses the best process and business practices of each subsidiary[8] as benchmarks for innovation. The firm has attempted to create an organisational structure and operating strategy that meet the twin goals of economic efficiency and localisation (see Chapter 7).

Determining strategic success and failure within firms

Across industries, certain firms stand out as consistently offering the latest and best products and services. Research by

McManus (1997) identified a number of pervasive values associated with global success and failure in re-engineering projects: leadership, core discipline, excellence and continuous improvement. The most frequently mentioned critical success factor in firms achieving global results today is effective leadership. Other key attributes included delivering a strong internal communications programme and vision, keeping focused on the goals and scope of the strategic initiative and making effective use of firm assets (Table 4.3).

One observation made is the link between high corporate ambition and success, in that having ambitious goals is more likely to produce results in the long term. However, as Peters and Waterman (1982) learned, having high ambition is not enough. Even when firms are at their peak and doing well the corporate culture is sometimes a detriment rather than a boost to initiatives, especially when budgets and power are at stake. In firms with excellent leaders, such as GE, Microsoft

Table 4.3   **Key attributes for success**

Attributes	Excellence	Intimacy	Leadership
Focus on process	Product life-cycle management Cost to market Continuous quality management Agile and lean operations	Relationship management Marketing and selling know-how Market alliances Price of ownership Product replacement strategies	Research and development Creative work and idea generation Communication and relationships Risk-reward coefficients
Focus on new ways to add value	Share product knowledge Reduce product overlaps One-to-one distribution	Lead-user rewards Share ownership and loyalty systems One-to-one marketing Online	Online customer development Accelerating learning curves Use of multimedia

and P&G, workers appear more empowered, make their own decisions and believe they are paid for innovation and performance. Information is more freely shared and there is a high risk-reward coefficient.

Michael Treacy and Fred Wiersema (1993) lay out a framework for understanding how firms achieve and sustain market success and leadership. The authors identify three characteristics for market leadership that emanate from a strategy built on operational excellence, customer intimacy and product leadership.

Operational excellence

Firms offer a convenient and reliable service or product at the optimum cost. Total cost encompasses price plus the cost of acquisition and the costs associated with any unreliability in the product or service. Today firms such McDonalds, Federal Express, UPS and Wal-Mart exhibit the characteristics of firms whose strategy is built on operational excellence and superior customer service.

Customer intimacy

Firms foster a loyal relationship with customers by providing a total solution to a customer need. They customise their service delivery by providing front-line teams with the necessary information to tailor decisions to specific customer needs. Customer-intimate companies focus on the quality and effectiveness of service delivery through the interpretation of customer requirements. They focus on lifetime customer profits, not earnings from a single transaction.

Direct Line, the UK insurer, invested £249 million in advertising in the 12 years until 2002. The result has been incredibly high brand recognition. The little red phone attracts 97 per cent identification with Direct Line and front-of-mind measures are now well ahead of rivals, with spontaneous brand awareness at 70 per cent compared to 54 per cent for its nearest competitor. A shift in strategy since 1995 has also paid dividends, providing the company with a broader competitive proposition. Not only is the price message still core, but also value and service scores are now ahead of its rivals.

Product leadership

Product leaders are the first to market a new product or service. These firms are willing to make a hefty investment in the unknown, knowing that certain customers will always pay more to have the best. They support innovation by establishing loose networks of people who learn and adapt by sharing ideas and information in the creative process. Product leadership companies exhibit responsiveness to changing market conditions through the communication of knowledge and ideas. Most of these firms are led by strong, inspirational leaders whose vision and passion drive the firm's business decisions. Such firms have a high tolerance for risk and are frequently willing to invest heavily in new products and technology before they have a clear indication of the pay-off.

For example, Nokia (Finland) has actively pursued a high economic integration and nationally responsive approach to customers and markets. A large degree of its success can be attributed to its R&D efforts, which have resulted in mobile phones that employ global roaming and allow the devices to be used across different telecommunications systems worldwide. Nokia has also been successful in forming alliances with other firms, such as AT&T, providing Nokia with access to large markets where it has successfully employed its product leadership strategies.

Key chapter messages

- Nations succeed in particular industries because their home environment is the most forward-looking, dynamic and challenging.

- The increasing dominance of BRIC nations is in many respects a direct consequence of ambitious national macroeconomic policies and business decisions taken in the last decade to improve economic conditions and resource utilisation.

- The competitive environment and the market forces inherent within it have become more hostile. Increasing competition from the BRIC nations and the globalisation of markets have combined to make business increasingly complex.

- A growing number of firms now meet the needs of segments-of-one in which the seller makes available a flexible market offering.

- Coping with emerging changes in technology, demographics, economics and distribution management requires a different approach to decision-making and thinking.

- An important trend regarding global competitiveness is the internationalisation of research and development and the inherent government forces which come into play. Today, the sources of competitive advantage of multinational enterprises do not lie in their home countries alone, but are spread over a number of locations and different countries.

- One of the major barriers to entry is spending on research and development. Heavy spending on R&D can act as a strong deterrent to potential entrants to any industry.

- Although the growth in innovation and entrepreneurship within the EU has brought many benefits to member countries, it has also created many challenges. In high-technology products, Europe's impressive inventive performance has not translated into overall market success.

- Seen in the context of the firm's strategy, the role of the CEO is to achieve superior performance relative to the competition. At the same time, the CEO must be sure that the underlying strategy accurately matches the strengths of the firm within the needs of a clearly defined market.

- The most frequently mentioned critical success factor in firms achieving global results is effective leadership. Other key attributes include delivering a strong internal communications programme and vision, keeping focused on the goals and scope of the strategic initiative and making effective use of the firm's assets.

Notes

1. That appointment launched his study of national, state and local competitiveness, the findings of which were first published in his book *The Competitive Advantage of Nations* in 1990.
2. In 1995 foreign companies' share of Brazil's exports and imports was less than 50 per cent, but by 2000 their share reached 60.4 per cent for exports and 56.6 per cent for imports. Foreign companies began to invest actively in Brazil by taking advantage of privatisation of public enterprises in 1996 and the strengthening of external competitiveness due to introducing more flexibility into the exchange rate in 1999.
3. According to a recent projection by Goldman Sachs (2003), Brazil will have overtaken Russia, the UK, Germany, France and Italy in GNP by 2050.
4. Personal discussion with Richard Heeks, 2005.
5. Philip Kotler in conversation with Paul Stonham, December 1994.

6. Tom Peters and Robert Waterman picked big companies considered 'innovative and excellent' in a variety of industries that had shown strong growth and profitability between 1961 and 1980.

7. The renewed emphasis on this classic brand icon and the resurrection of the 'Enjoy' slogan seemed to be a fitting way for a US – if not global – institution to launch itself into the new millennium. However, the company ended 1999 with the surprising news that the beleaguered Ivester would retire in early 2000 after just two-and-a-half years at the helm – a tenure marked perhaps most tellingly by seven straight quarters of earnings decline. Taking over was Douglas N. Daft, a native Australian and 30-year Coke veteran who had headed the company's operating group covering the Middle and Far East and Africa; he was named president and chief operating officer in December 1999 before becoming chairman and CEO the following February.

8. Most of the products are produced or assembled in P&G-owned facilities, with 10 per cent at third-party manufacturers.

5

Emergent global and international business strategies

Emergent strategy: rethinking the paradigm

The concept of strategy and strategic thinking applied to business is in many ways a legacy of old primary and secondary industries which were heavily reliant on labour and infrastructure. Alfred Chandler (1965), a business historian, traces the roots of modern management to the origins of the US railroad business in the mid-nineteenth century. The nature of the railways dictated a need for central means of control but with localised management of operations – which became the genesis of decentralisation. Perhaps the most influential writer on strategy in the last half of the twentieth century was Igor Ansoff (1990), whose treatise on corporate strategy set out a practical methodology for successfully formulating and implementing strategy. Its essence is that most strategic decisions are made within a restricting framework of resources and are therefore limited to a choice of alternatives. It could be argued that such decisions rely on 'continuity', where the objective is to produce a resource allocation which offers the best potential for meeting the firm's objectives.

In recent years writers such as Henry Mintzberg (1994) have been influential in offering the global business community a strategic paradigm based on 'discontinuity'. The real challenge in crafting today's strategies lies in the firm's ability to detect subtle discontinuities that may undermine an organisation in the future. Such discontinuities are unexpected and irregular, essentially exceptional. They can be dealt with only by minds that are attuned to existing patterns yet able to perceive important breaks in them. So who do these minds belong to? Who are the strategists? Most of the literature on strategic management as well as the popular press has an answer to the question of who is responsible for strategy: the chief executive. Chief executives like Joe McGrath of Unisys, who reinvented the organisation within 18 months of taking over as CEO in 2005. McGrath went to the board with an ambitious plan to transform the company. The strategy focused on Unisys's 'innovation and technological strengths'. The plan was to focus its services and solutions portfolio on five fast-growing market segments. In 2005 Unisys was operating in 50 countries, but 80 per cent of its business came out of ten countries. Unisys pared down investment in smaller markets, cutting 15 per cent of its employee base, moving jobs overseas and retraining employees on its top five agenda (*DM Review*, 2005). Today, 10 per cent of its employees are offshore, in countries like India, China and Hungary. McGrath's goal is to have 20 per cent of people offshore by the end of 2008. The Unisys strategy called for reinforcing the company's network of client engagement delivery centres in key locations around the globe. It planned to develop integrated horizontal competency (innovation) centres and geographically centralise its delivery resources to complement its focal growth areas, maximising the skills available to create and deliver solutions for clients.

Like McGrath, other chief executives (and their managers) are now facing similar challenges within their organisations and markets. As emphasised in a recent IBM survey (IBM, 2006), some 65 per cent of chief executives and other business leaders agree that they will have to make fundamental changes in their business strategies over the next few years. A key message coming out of many boardrooms is that innovation is indispensable. One of the report's key findings is that business model innovation is becoming the new strategic differentiator, and the model organisations ultimately choose will determine and influence the success or failure of their strategy. A key driver here is the need to address unexpected market shifts and demographic changes. In effect, CEOs and their managers must engage on multiple levels where 'old' and 'new' ways of doing business coincide with one another. According to Mintzberg (1994), in the new paradigm strategies – often initially modest and even obscure – emerge as the people who develop the products and deliver the services solve little problems that merge into new initiatives (Table 5.1).

Sustaining new and innovative strategic business is tough to accomplish without financial backing and time. Time is a competitive weapon in getting the product or service to market, and getting immediate feedback is seen by many CEOs as a major business benefit. According to the IBM (2006) survey, strategic innovation allows companies to specialise and move more quickly to seize emerging growth opportunities. Overall, CEOs' rankings suggest that business model innovation is helping their organisations to become more nimble and responsive, while at the same time lowering costs. One CEO explained: 'Innovating with respect to business models and operations will not only create opportunities for cost savings, but will also lead to additional revenue generation opportunities.' The combination

Table 5.1 Emergent thinking in strategy

Strategy present paradigm Focus is on markets and closed business models	Strategy emerging paradigm Focus is on innovation and open business models
Clear, deliberate and bold Emanates from CEO, who takes the dramatic acts that drive up share price Managers implement	Often initially modest and even obscure Emerges as people who develop products and deliver services etc. solve little problems that merge into new initiatives

Drivers
    Shareholder value
    Market share
    Customer satisfaction
    Fixed-cost reduction
    Performance
    Quality
    Skills
    Patents
    Shared risk
    Centralised decision-making
    Improvement based on market
    feedback
    Stakeholder involvement
    Short-term partnerships
    Technology focused
	Drivers
	    Shareholder value
	    Velocity faster time to markets
	    High quantity of customer
	    retention
	    Move to variable costs
	    Shared risk
	    Shared intellectual property
	    Capability retention
	    Labour innovation
	    Small-scale infrastructure
	    Decentralised decision-making
	    Stakeholders as assets
	    Sustained partnerships
	    Incremental adjustments
	    based on customer feedback
	    Information focused

of pressures from market risk, competition and innovation should power many firms into revisiting their strategic business models (Figure 5.1).

According to Chesbrough (2006: 2), one development which underpins this emerging paradigm is the growing division of innovation of labour. The term 'innovation of labour' is a system where one party develops an idea but does not carry this idea to market itself. Instead, that party partners with or sells the idea to another party, and this party carries the idea to market. One weakness within the existing strategic paradigm is that once a company develops

Figure 5.1 **Emerging strategic pressures**

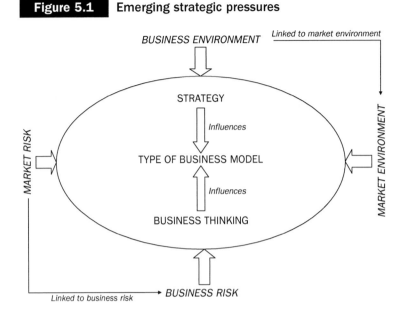

an innovative strategy, it shifts its attention and emphasis to improving this strategy to make it better. Little or no attention is given to discovering new ways of innovating. This is especially the case with successful companies.

Constantinos Markides distinguishes between complementary and disruptive strategic innovation (Mang, 2000). The latter is innovation that threatens the existing way of doing business, and as a result is not very popular with established companies. Markides suggests that perhaps established companies can wait until somebody else comes up with an idea, and then move to adopt the disruptive innovation and scale it up. To him, the ability to scale up an idea is as innovative and important as coming up with the idea in the first place. He also proposes that to scale up such a disruptive innovation, the firm may want to separate the innovation into a different unit. However, he stresses that while separation has its advantages, it also has disadvantages. Firms need to decide whether or not they will do this based on their individual circumstances.

Business models and management metaphors

As previously stated, the pace of doing business is accelerating – entire industries are today engaged in a war against apathy and unwanted delays. High-technology firms are under pressure to roll out new products and services in months, not years. Firms reaping the greatest performance gains are not simply automating existing processes and procedures or benchmarking the achievements of others, but fundamentally rethinking the role of their business models with an eye towards greatly increasing their value-added activities. The pressures to improve business performance have never been stronger – whether it is inventory turnover, the rate at which you have to introduce innovation or the means by which firms generate revenues, the message is the same:

- find new ways to add value;
- focus on business models;
- find new business metaphors;
- rethink business assumptions.

Although new products and services remain a goal for many firms, the need for differentiation through innovation is now the new Holy Grail. A decade ago organisations such as Delta Airlines led the way in financial business engineering, doing away with budgeting in favour of asset-allocation decisions. Today, just rethinking financial processes is not good enough. Firms must rethink the whole business paradigm; unlike business process re-engineering, where you could replicate ways of doing things or business processes, it is more difficult to copy a business model because it is much more complex.

Alexander Osterwalder[1] cites the example of Apple and its success with the iPod. The success does not come from the iPod product, but from a whole bundle of things, including the iTunes software. According to Osterwalder, this is a good example of business model innovation. It is not just product innovation of an MP3 player that is powerful and elegantly designed. There are a lot of rival products in the field, but it is much more difficult to recall their names. Despite having quite powerful products, competitors do not have a business model to match that of Apple. Even if they have more powerful products than Apple, Apple won the market through its business model, not the iPod itself. After the introduction of the iPod, Apple's revenues grew from US$5.3 billion in 2001 to $13.9 billion in 2005; over the same period, its share price rose 305 per cent from less than $10 to over $40.

Henry Chesbrough (quoted in *Computing Business*, 2007) suggests that a business model is a story. It is the story of how a firm makes money. The problem with stories is that the more they are told the more sacred they become. A company may focus on its core business, but if it does not repeatedly challenge the logic of its business model, its revenue streams will dry up. According to Ballon (2006), a business model defines the architecture of the product or service, the roles and relations of the company and its customers, partners and suppliers, and the physical, virtual and financial flows between them. To achieve this level of integration firms 'must' synchronise the three cornerstones of the business model: capital structure, cost structure and revenue structure (Figure 5.2). While firms often initiate efforts to improve the efficiency of their business models,

Figure 5.2 Three cornerstones of business models

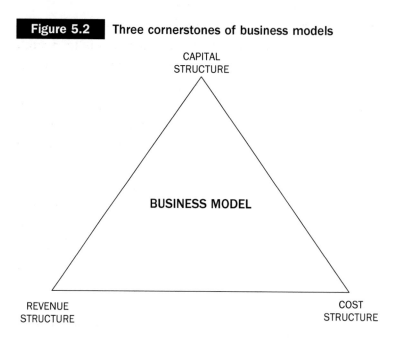

CAPITAL
STRUCTURE

BUSINESS MODEL

REVENUE
STRUCTURE

COST
STRUCTURE

they soon discover that gains in one attribute (for example, revenue) may be lost through dysfunctional cost systems and structure. Equally, managers may not have the vision or mindset to implement successfully what is important to the business.

Metaphors are often used to assist expression or understanding of business or business language. For example, managers may use the expression 'I'm comfortable with my decision' (*the mind is a physical thing: mental pain = physical pain*). Managers often use sufficing strategies to avoid taking sole ownership for difficult decisions. This lack of ownership is the single biggest hurdle to creating an efficient, streamlined business. Complex, non-integrated business models spawn inconsistent strategies and waste. Charles Simpson[2] tells a story of one client which sold large capital equipment such as graders and diggers. This client believed its core business was selling capital equipment. In a strategy review Simpson identified that the real high-margin opportunities (*revenue structure*) were actually in the rental, leasing and product support business. The mindset shift was the biggest challenge for this organisation. Simpson noted that it perceived itself as a seller of large bits of metal, yet all the bottom-line impact came from intangible services. In this organisation there was a lack of flexibility, which made it difficult to realign its resources (*cost structure*) and focus (*ownership*) on the real business opportunity.

The drive to find new ways to add value is often premised not just on finding or inventing a new business model, but in large-scale change. Before such change can take place the management must agree on two key issues: a vision of the way the firm will operate in the future, and the means by which it is achieved (which must exert a strong push). When Proctor and Gamble was looking to recover from its poor share value and market position in 2000, it needed to move from a closed model of business to one that was more open and flexible. In 2001 P&G underwent a dramatic business transformation, adopting open innovation and an open business model. It called the programme Connect and Develop. The main objective was to look outside P&G's corporate walls to find new products, technology, packaging, design, processes and business models.

One of P&G's strengths is its network of technology entrepreneurs who scour the globe for new ideas. It focuses its resources on specific countries for specific solutions. P&G's open business model allows it the flexibility to learn from other industries and take this domain knowledge into competitor markets. Using this strategy P&G can enable its operations to compete more cost-efficiently. Under the new business model, anyone with a good business idea can approach P&G to take the innovation to market. Some of the new products that have emerged from the Connect and

Develop programme include Olay Regenerist, the Swifter Duster and Mr Clean Magic Eraser. Today P&G has 36,000 patents and more than 60,000 trademarks globally. It has a vast technology portfolio in chemistry, materials and biosciences, as well as know-how in information technology, manufacturing and consumer research.

Recursive causality in strategic management

For many organisations the strategic choices they make will invariably influence their success or failure in the marketplace. According to Magretta (quoted in Jansen et al., 2007: 7):

> The creation of a business model strongly resembles the writing of a new story. To a certain extent of course all new stories are variations to older stories. They are new versions of the universal themes on which human experiences are based. Similarly, all new business models are variations to the general value chain that forms the basis of all businesses.

In this sense, organisations must have the vision and courage to change and move value into the marketplace. Proctor and Gamble realised it was stuck within a value chain that was weak – it needed to reinvent itself. Collaboration was a key element of P&G's growth strategy and business strategy. In achieving its turnaround P&G paid attention to what Dutta and Segev (1999) call the 'market space'. In market space, two dimensions are important: the technological capacity dimension and the strategic business dimension. The strategic business dimension of the market space is based on the classical marketing model of the four Ps (product, price, promotion and placement). In essence the model is typical and recursive in many organisations. The marketing view supporting this recursive model is competition. Although a good starting point, the real leverage comes from knowing and understanding your customers.

It could be argued that a well-conceived strategy is based on understanding the importance of 'the customer' and not the strategic game itself. Despite the overwhelming theory of management and its application to contemporary business models in the last two decades, little has been learnt to counter the ongoing business failures in many international markets. While we have witnessed new means of conducting business, the fundamentals of competition remain unchanged. As noted by Jack Welch (2005: 165):

> it's not that I don't understand their theories (strategy) about competitive advantage, core competencies, virtual commerce, supply chain economics, disruptive innovation, and so on, it's just that the way these experts tend to talk about strategy – as if it is some kind of high-brain scientific methodology – feels really off to me.

When Welch became CEO of GE in 1981, he launched a highly publicised initiative which aimed to make GE number one or number two in each of its markets. Welch says this was a galvanising mantra to describe how GE was going to do business. If a company has a problem to solve, one way to look at it would be to identify if any other company in the world had solved part of the problem. It is a strategy that has been used to great effect in GE, and overturns the conventional notion of strategy. In this way Welch moved

GE's business model from commoditised to high-value service and products. GE's business model was and is highly dependent on the degree of interoperability and competency (ideas and innovation to markets). One of Welch's legacies is that GE today is a wealthy organisation which knows its customers, markets and internal strengths and weaknesses.

The consumer interface

The application of a recursive strategic model within a growing and sophisticated consumer economy raises some interesting questions about who is the customer and how we retain him. On what in the customer's world – economy, business, market – do we depend? Is it economics? Is it such trends as the constant shifts from commoditisation to services, from low price to high convenience in an affluent society? What is the outlook? And are we geared to take advantage of the factors favourable to us? What are the meaningful aggregates in the customer's mind and in his economy? What makes them aggregates?

In order to answer these questions we have to put ourselves in a transcendental state and be at one with the customer. Centralising the customer within our own universe provides a powerful insight for both parties. As an example, Margaret Neville (2004) tells the following story:

> I was reading an interesting piece on Southwest airlines and what they have named their 'Warrior Spirit.' The original founder of Southwest, Herb Kelleher, knew nothing about airlines but knew a lot about justice, fair play, mission and spirit. Because of him and his leadership he instilled 'fire in the bellies' of his employees. Southwest was the only airline to record a profit in 2001.

In contrast Simon Martin, client director at AT&T, was tasked with building a relationship with one of the world's largest oil companies, with which AT&T had no business. Historically, the oil company saw AT&T as bureaucratic, slow and chunky, and a company that did business in the USA. Martin developed a strategy which focused on increasing revenue and building relationships. The motto here is that all successful strategies are very simple. Building customer relationships is the cornerstone to building business: without relationships it is very difficult to achieve anything. The key is doing what you say you are going to do.

Creative approaches to innovative business strategies

In the process of managing relationships one often encounters new ways of doing business which redefine the way the strategic game is played. Companies such as Ryanair, Starbucks and Amazon have become successful by changing the rules of the game. Starbucks, for example, turned the coffee industry upside-down by shifting its focus from commodity coffee sales to the emotional experience enjoyed by customers drinking their coffee. When Howard Schultz launched Starbucks with a few coffee-shops in Seattle, few realised that a new competitor had been born. At the heart of Starbucks's early success was its customer relationship management strategy. Schultz's unrestrained confidence, obsessive attention to detail and focus on quality earned him a loyal customer following among America's middle class and campus students. Success, however, can breed complacency, and by being content with yourself you lose the edge and intensity that got you where you are in the first place. A recent communication from Howard Schultz[3] to Starbucks's executives highlights this issue of complacency:

> rapid expansion, the chairman, Howard Schultz, said, has led to a 'commoditization of our brand' that makes the company more vulnerable to competitors. Specifically, he cited several decisions that, he said, may have been right at the time, but which, in retrospect, have led to a 'dilution' of the coffeehouse experience that he wanted to foster.

This statement reflects one issue that Mr Schultz has identified over the years – the delicate balance between expanding into a global brand while maintaining the intimate communal experience that led to Starbucks's early success. The truth is that market leaders often think themselves invincible. Companies should look inward, for there lie the greatest danger and the greatest opportunity.

The challenge here is relevance and currency: few strategies survive a brush with reality. Opportunism is increasingly driving business innovation and change, and strategy is more and more a tool which helps CEOs to justify how they respond to a threat or an opportunity rather than a means of identifying those threats and opportunities. The idea here is not primarily to knock out the competition. It is about inventing games that are played outside the traditional boundaries. Unless a firm is able to think in completely new ways, and to move beyond what is accepted industry practice, it will not be able to flee head-to-head competition with its competitors. This is the means to develop new ideas and expand the portfolio to include new customers that competitors are not even looking at.

Some of the greatest business opportunities in recent times have come in the world of e-business. A 2002 Information Technology Online (ITOL) research report commissioned by the Australian National Office of the Information Economy concluded:

> What we are witnessing in contemporary organisational life is the transformative opportunities wrought by technological changes, most recently through web-based technology and the Internet, shaking traditional foundations of organising and the very nature of organisations. Within such a context, organisational relationships, especially collaboration, is a crucial issue. While 'we' have seen a more than steady growth in collaborative activity around the globe over the past decade or so, developments in technology, and, particularly, in e-business (or online business) seem to have escalated that growth. (McGrath and More, 2002: 1)

A recent survey by Jupiter Research estimates that consumers spend around 10 per cent of their money online and that online advertising is now a $16 billion business in the USA (Pratt, 2002). In 2008 it is predicted that some $900 million will be spent on social networking sites in America. The role of online communities has become increasingly important to the success of e-business. The e-business enterprise's capacity for creativity and ability to leverage the community will determine if it loses or wins in the market space. Commercial success in e-business depends on organising and exploiting the potential of virtual communities. The key argument is based on the premise that the knowledge, content and resources produced by online communities are extremely valuable commodities.

According to Chesbrough (2008), firms must search for useful technologies (means and ways) that can advance their business model from any sources that can provide the appropriate opportunities at the right time. When ideas connect directly to a company's business model, they create additional power and leverage for other parts of the strategy. For example, Facebook, the 'social network' site started by Mark Zuckerberg, is inventing new ways of reaching consumers and as such is attracting mature businesses like Coca-Cola, Conde Nast, General Motors, Nike and a host of other world-famous brand names to its site. The move away from traditional models of advertising such as television, newspapers and other media to internet-based models has assisted many companies in reaching a wider and diversified consumer-based audience. Internet businesses collect a lot of personal data about their customers. Social network sites such as Facebook bring consumers together in ways that the traditional models do not. Consumers share their taste in music, books and films, their political views and their location. All this information can potentially be turned into well-targeted advertising and consumer strategies.

A word of caution, though: firms need to remember that e-business (the internet) is a two-way street. The bursting of the dot.com bubble in 2000, in which US markets lost $2 trillion in value, ushered in an era of renewed interest in business management of information technology and the so-called business and technology disconnect. Technology and business can sometimes make poor bedfellows. For evidence, look to those companies and their investors that lost millions in the last dot.com wave. Boo.com, originally founded in the UK in 1998 as an online fashion store, was beset with problems and mismanagement from the start. Its complicated website was very slow to load at a time when dial-up internet usage was the norm. Boo spent millions marketing itself as a global company, but then had to deal with different languages, pricing and tax structures in all the countries it served. The company also furtively decided to pay postage on returns, but, even more importantly, sales never reached expectations. Boo.com eventually went through $160 million before liquidation in May 2000. Technology start-ups are often convinced they understand the markets and the needs of customers. Often these companies do not know how to manage strong growth or transition. When Google bought YouTube, the video-sharing website, there was a lot of complaining from users. Some lessons have, however, been learned: unlike in the first internet boom, the big media corporations have in the main stopped paying huge prices for online firms.

Emergent innovation and strategic transfer mechanisms

The absorption rates of technological innovation are forever accelerating the time to reach critical mass (say 10 million consumers); for many new products and services the period is less than 12 months. The convergence of new technologies has helped forge new business models in many intermediate markets where suppliers license know-how and intellectual property to downstream developers and producers – no more so than in mobile technology, where suppliers, developers and end users work in a symbiotic relationship. In strategic and economic terms the profits lie within the metadata of new emerging technologies like mobile communications, wireless, broadband and satellite services. As high bandwidth emerges, with potential to provide more than just voice services on mobile phones, the most advanced markets will provide a testing ground for new services and their market potential.

Within the intermediate mobile service markets we have witnessed a significant amount of innovation (for example the development of voice-over-internet protocols – VoIP[4]). Within the mobile services industry there are moves to develop packages of services tailored to individual consumer needs. In economic terms, the central feature of the mobile services industry is the provider's ability to manipulate, store and transmit large quantities of information (or service packets) at low cost.

An equally important feature of these new technologies is their pervasiveness. The growing shift towards using the internet to provide phonecalls, web access, films on demand, digital TV and, ultimately, fixed-mobile convergence where mobiles can access home connectivity and make calls even when travelling presents a number of strategic and business challenges. The question within many of the intermediate and secondary telecommunications markets is how to generate new revenue streams in areas where the average revenue per user is falling. One answer seems to be in service diversification. Google, the commercial search engine provider, has two core strategies: to reinforce its existing revenue base, keep pushing ahead and avoid becoming outmanoeuvred by competitors; and to find new revenue streams. Google's business model is based on providing information services to customers that it can advertise around the globe to deliver value added to its shareholders. Google is currently looking to diversify its operations into mobile processing, exploring ways and means to move away from the desktop. According to Peter Norvig, 'in the developing world we're seeing a trend towards skipping the desktop and moving directly towards mobile phones as the main means of communication' (Kelly, 2007). Google's future strategy possibly lies in brokering mobile content; it also has ambitions to move into micro transactions and micro payments using the Checkout service. If Google gets its payment system into the mobile channel it will provide a serious revenue stream for the company.

Aligning technology and business

Economic growth and productivity are increasingly determined by the rate of technological innovation and the means by which this innovation is applied within the business model. Innovation has always come from individuals and firms that have chosen to take a leap because of who they are, not because they were taught to innovate in some way. Firms that adapt their business models and integrate new technologies within their core activities tend to expand and grow their market faster than those that do not. Being open to technologies that are not inputs to the company but are still complementary to the core activities of the firm makes good business sense.

For example, Pacific Coast Producers, which sells $400 million of packaged and canned fruit annually to Wal-Mart and other grocers under various brand names, got together early with Wal-Mart's radio frequency identification tagging mandate. As a result Pacific Coast Producers has created a cross-functional team of information knowledge workers and sales and customer service employees who work with Wal-Mart on ways to improve the supply chain and ultimately boost the supplier's sales. Aligning information technology meticulously with external and internal customers' needs is now the end game for astute firms.

Another example is Jimmy Choo, the footwear and accessories specialist, which recently implemented a multi-protocol label-switching network that guaranteed an identical look and feel across the organisation. The network enables all applications and communications, and any employee can be reached through a four-digit extension under a simple global dial plan. If staff are not at their desks, calls are automatically forwarded to their mobiles. The network also links data, collected twice daily from each store, to two separate data centres. As a result the firm can now open new stores in just two weeks, and plans to have more than 200 stores across the globe by 2009.

These stories illustrate the emergence of an important force that is shaping and effecting global markets, and that force is innovation.

Key chapter messages

- Most strategic decisions are made within a restricting framework of resources and are therefore limited to a choice of alternatives.

- Innovation is becoming the new strategic differentiator, and the business model organisations choose will ultimately determine and influence the success or failure of their strategy.

- Time is a competitive weapon in getting the product or service to market, and getting immediate feedback is a major business benefit.

- One weakness within the existing strategic paradigm is that once a company develops an innovative strategy, it shifts its attention and emphasis to improving this strategy to make it better. Little or no attention is given to discovering new ways of innovating. This is especially the case with successful companies.

- Firms are under pressure to roll out new products and services in months, not years.

- A company may focus on its core business, but if it does not repeatedly challenge the logic of its business model, its revenue streams will dry up.

- Firms must have the vision and courage to change and move value into the marketplace.

- Market leaders often think themselves invincible. Companies should look inward, for there lie the greatest danger and the greatest opportunity.

- Firms must search for useful technologies (means and ways) that can advance their business model from any sources that can provide the appropriate opportunities at the right time.

- Innovation has always come from individuals and firms which have chosen to take a leap because of who they are, not because they were taught to innovate in some way.

Notes

1. Dr Alexander Osterwalder is managing partner at Arvetica, Geneva.
2. Charles Simpson is a partner with PA Consulting Group.
3. The memorandum was sent on 14 February 2007, and appears on the website www.starbucksgossip.com.
4. VoIP is voice and data transmission that goes over telephone wires but, like the internet, sends information in packets. This gives all kinds of benefits, from cost reduction (like the web, it is telephony always on) and mobile identities (logging in becomes a matter of just plug-and-play) to call quality (so-called hi-fi telephony).

6

Managing the strategic process in a global and international business environment

Determining the strategic process

As discussed in the last chapter, successful firms are those that have the vision and courage to challenge existing business models and develop innovative ways to bring value to the market more efficiently and effectively than the competition. The courage element will be discussed later in this chapter, but let us consider the vision issue first.

It is often argued that much of business success is dependent upon luck and good fortune. Many CEOs have been credited with saying 'Lucky? Of course I'm lucky – I spend 18 hours a day making sure I am lucky.' Vision and foresight are only developed through hard work and a large amount of research. The existence of a clearly articulated and shared vision of the desired future is a prerequisite for a successful organisation. That vision must be a compelling story that all departments and levels of an organisation can accept and believe to be achievable. In *The Power of the Tale*, Julie Allan et al. (2002) describe the use of stories in corporate life, and even in the development of policy within countries (Le Roux, 1997). The authors tell us that stories work because they are memorable, economical and entertaining, and they are centred on people. They also encourage creativity, help in handling emotions, help to make sense of puzzling or ambiguous situations and co-evolve with an organisation's culture.

According to Jack Welch (2005), in real life strategy is very straightforward. You pick a general direction and implement like hell. Finding the right direction can be agonising, so it generally pays off to plan within a framework using broad scenarios. Scenarios are about communication, and are the best way to handle complexity, ambiguity, uncertainty and rapid change, all features of the global and international business environment. Peter Schwartz (1991), founder of the Global Business Network – possibly the most famous scenario-planning organisation since the death of Herbert Kahn – has said that there is no one perfect way to create scenarios. The process is not about imagining a future that you like and then believing it will happen; it is about imagining possible futures and ensuring that the firm develops sufficient capability and flexibility to deal with elements of the scenarios that emerge.

The last decade has seen considerable world changes. The impact of future changes in the external environment upon a firm cannot be overestimated, and the organisation's response can be critical to its success and even its survival. The oil industry is enjoying a changing relationship with the Russian organisations with which it has partnered to develop and exploit some of the richest oil and gas fields currently available (Pappe and Drankina, 2007). To a large extent, this changing relationship is due to the increasing power being exercised by the Russian government. Although the privatisation of the Russian oil industry reached completion in 2003 with the distribution of power between four private companies, Yukos, LUKOil, TNK-BP and Surgutneftgaz, subsequent acquisitions and changes when the oil prices reached $80 a barrel mean that the state has become a far bigger presence in the industry. The three trends which have led to this, and which might have been anticipated by scenario planning, are a desire by officials to strengthen the role of the state in a strategic industry, resentment towards Yukos and societal confidence in the justice of the privatisation process.

Yukos was returned to state ownership via the vehicle of 'unpaid taxes'. By various routes Yukos's assets became the property of Rozneft. Together with the state-controlled Gazprom and the 10 per cent of Rozneft owned by the government through an intermediary, the Russian government now controls more than 50 per cent of the assets of a number of ventures in the energy industry. In the last three years Gazprom has acquired controlling packets of Sakhalin II, Russia Petroleum (the Kovyktin deposit), Nortgaza, Salavatnefteorgsinteza and Mosenergo and 19.9 per cent of Novatek, the largest independent producer of natural gas. Two other wholesale generating companies (WGCs) and the largest producer of carbon fuels, Siberian Carbon Fuel Firm, are preparing to be taken over by Gazprom. Complaints have been filed against Chayanlinskoye natural gas deposit and one of the Sakhalin III projects. Moreover, Gazprom is actively using its authoritarian resources: too often a buyout will be preceded by ecological or tax complaints, threats to withdraw licences, etc.

Changes in the nature of competition because of new entrants or new business models may also be a feature of the environment that creates a strategic issue. As will be seen in the case study in Chapter 8, the competitive landscape in the airline industry in India has changed dramatically with the launch of Air Deccan, a low-cost airline similar to Ryanair and Easyjet. At the time the airline launched, in 2003, there were two state-controlled airlines in India – Indian Airlines, serving the domestic market, and Air India, serving the international sector. Captain Gorur Ramaswamy Gopinath, co-founder and CEO of Air Deccan, said:

> Air travel was, for a long time, a fantasy for Indians. There was a cost factor. Only the rich could afford it. There was also a social factor, uniquely Indian. A handyman, for example, was expected to travel on duty only by road or rail, however urgent the need. A CEO or senior bureaucrat was expected to travel only by air, however trivial the purpose. What is occurring today is a change of expectations, a democratisation of travel. Air travel in India, in that sense, has been a market waiting to happen. Air Deccan broke the barriers of perception. That is why it has succeeded. (Gopinath, 2004)

Air Deccan had the vision of being 'the preferred airline of air travellers in India' and its mission was 'to demystify air travel in India by providing reliable, low-cost air travel to the common man by constantly driving down air fares'.[1] The trends that could have been identified that brought about this change to the competitive environment were the growth in the Indian economy, the rising expectations of the IT élite of India and the recognition by the Indian government of the need to liberalise the airline industry to add further growth to the economy (Gupta, 2006).

Determining strategic formulation and dynamics

The strategy that an organisation follows emerges from a number of drivers. There will be a deliberate strategic intent mandated by senior management or powerful external stakeholders (such as national governments), but by the time that strategy is realised there will have been adaptations caused by other drivers or factors. Those factors could include the actions of staff and employees at other levels in the firm, agents outside the organisation or any number of others who interpret the strategy through their own strategic lens. The combination of these factors leads to the delivered strategy emerging from the actions of a number of different stakeholders.

What is important is that the organisation, or at least the powerful coalitions within it, has a clear idea of where it wants to be at some time in the future and can put strategies in place to have a chance of getting reasonably close to that desired outcome. The clarity of the strategies devised will make the implementation process that much easier. A good strategy does not necessarily make for a good outcome, but a poor strategy will always lead to a poor outcome – no matter how well the implementation process is carried out. Contrast the fortunes of two American steel companies, Nucor and Bethlehem Steel. Nucor had highly developed technological capabilities, was a first mover and initial adopter of the thin-slab-casting process for producing flat-rolled steel developed by SMS in Germany and rapidly built plants close to the demand for steel – the Midwest of America. It operated with a flat organisational structure and recognised the importance of people by operating a meritocracy, differentiating itself from the rest of the steel industry. Bethlehem, by contrast, was slow to adopt new technology, insisted on keeping to its old, established plants, many in landlocked locations, operated a tall, very hierarchical structure and did not enjoy good labour relations. Today, Bethlehem Steel is a distant memory, with some of its assets bought out of bankruptcy by Nucor (Collins, 2001).

Similar results were seen at Wells Fargo, which operated like a mini-Citicorp – and not a very good one at that. Having asked themselves 'what can we, potentially, do better than any other firm?', Wells Fargo realised it would never be the best bank in the world. Recognising that in a deregulated world commercial banking would become a commodity, it realised that profit per employee would be far more important than profit per loan. The leadership team pulled the plug on the vast majority of the bank's international operations, and it switched to becoming a pioneering leader in electronic banking and opening utilitarian branches run by small crews of superb people. Profit per employee skyrocketed. Finally, when it came to passion, members of the Wells Fargo team all agreed: the mindless waste and self-awarded perks of traditional banking culture were revolting. They proudly saw themselves as stoic Spartans in an industry that had been dominated by a wasteful, élitist culture. The Wells Fargo team eventually translated their vision into a simple, well-articulated concept: run a bank like a business, with a focus on the western USA, and consistently increase profit per employee. 'Run it like a business' and 'run it like you own it' became mantras; simplicity and focus made all the difference. With fanatical adherence to that simple idea, Wells Fargo made the leap from good results to superior results (Clarke, 2001).

Determining strategic choice (entry and exit strategies)

Selecting overseas markets and the mode of entry is a critical issue for any organisation which aspires to operate globally. As the need for a global presence and the intensity of competition increase, the importance of the decisions to be made also increases significantly. There are a number of components to the overall decision:

- the objectives and goals in the selected target market;
- the choice of target market/country;
- the choice of entry mode to penetrate the market;
- the control system to monitor performance in the selected market.

However, it has been argued that two of these decisions are not in fact separate (Koch, 2001), and that selecting the target market and selecting the mode of entry are decisions that should be taken together. Whether this is true or not, there are considerations that need to be made under each element of the joint decision. The choice of market can be described under three broad headings: strategic elements; extent of national differences; and extent of scale economies and global concentration. These variables will help a firm decide whether to adopt a truly 'global' strategy or a 'multidomestic' strategy. A multidomestic strategy is appropriate when there is evidence that national markets differ sufficiently in respect of consumer tastes and preferences, competitive and operating conditions and political, legal and social structures. To be successful a multinational will assign key operating and strategic responsibilities to national subsidiaries, each with its own marketing approach and autonomous production facilities, and the competitive strategy will reflect local conditions. The corporate centre will exercise a relatively low degree of control over the subsidiaries. This may well mean that the preferred mode of entry will be via a joint venture or alliance as a lower-cost alternative.

However, in many industries the ubiquity of modern communications and the increasing rapidity of transport systems have caused a convergence in tastes and preferences of consumers in an increasing number of nations (Levitt, 1983). This has resulted in enormous global markets for standardised products, leading to scale economies for those companies that can capitalise upon them by centralising production and adopting a single marketing message. These homogeneous market conditions exist in a number of industries, notably aerospace, heavy construction equipment, watches, semiconductors, computers and heavy electrical equipment. A firm will configure its value chain so as to maximise value at every stage. Each national subsidiary may well be responsible for only one part of the manufacturing process, exchanging components with other national subsidiaries, with final assembly being completed near to the market being served. To some extent this is being done by both Boeing and Airbus, as will be seen in the case study in Chapter 8, although in both firms final assembly is completed in the home country since the end product can fly to its market.

A further example is that of Ford, which pioneered the concept of the 'world car' (Malkin, 1994). The second-largest US automaker will now run its operations from five centres, each responsible for the worldwide manufacturing, sales, design, development and supply of specific models. The coordination of interdependent global manufacturing requires a high degree of control over the operations of the different national subsidiaries. Where the firm is operating in an industry that is already concentrated, with few players, it may enter the home market of a rival to limit that rival's ability to compete globally. So in a market that is already globally concentrated, market entry may be purely defensive, to focus a competitor's attention on its home market and limit its willingness to expand further overseas. When Fuji entered the US market, which Kodak believed to be its own, Kodak immediately opened a subsidiary in Japan and sold film at very low prices to damage Fuji's share of its home market. Although

Kodak was making a loss on its Japanese operations, it considered this worth it to limit Fuji's further expansion. This strategy worked until the WTO ruled against Kodak and the US government in their complaint that the Japanese government was unfairly limiting access to the Japanese market (Deutsch, 1997). This strategy required a high degree of central control.

Historically, where market risk is considered to be high the firm will attempt to limit its resource exposure, and alliances or joint ventures will be preferred to outright ownership of subsidiaries; it may even limit itself to licensing agreements. In the event of joint ventures, it may be that the local partner has some influence over government departments or political parties and, with a vested interest, can prevent appropriation of assets. The location familiarity will reflect the perceived distance between the home and target countries in terms of culture and accepted business practice. Shorter perceived distances arise by virtue of the quality of the firm's past experience of the culture and country. The shorter the perceived distance, the more likely the firm is to form a closer working relationship, and this will favour the establishment of a fully owned subsidiary; conversely, the greater the distance the more likely the move towards licensing and a looser relationship.

Hofstede (1991) has written extensively on the perceived distance between cultures. His classification discusses the extent to which different cultures accept the asymmetry of power distribution, the degree of individualism, the degree of the importance of masculinity and the degree of uncertainty avoidance. Combining these four factors will provide a ranking of countries in terms of their dominant behaviour. While the UK and USA are grouped together as 'egalitarian individualists', China, India and Brazil are described as 'hierarchical collectivists' and sit in the opposite quadrant of Hofstede's (1980) grid. There is therefore a 'liability of foreignness', which a multinational firm will incur compared to local firms when it chooses to operate overseas. This can manifest itself through the firm's unfamiliarity with the foreign environment, discriminatory attitudes of customers, local suppliers, governments and others and additional costs of operating internationally. This liability will not be the same for all foreign firms choosing to enter a market, and Hofstede's work gives an indication of the degree to which a firm will be affected.

Aside from the need for there to be sufficient demand to make entry into a market worthwhile, the firm will be influenced in its decision by the certainty of those demand conditions. The level of resource commitment will be dependent upon both high demand and relatively high certainty about that demand. This will be affected by the position in the life cycle of the industry, with embryonic and end-of-life industries attracting lower resource commitments in general. Similarly, the volatility of the competition will affect how a firm chooses to enter the market, since a high resource commitment will limit the firm's strategic flexibility in the event of attracting intense competition. The model outlined in Figure 6.1 suggests the process that should be used for selection of both country and mode of entry.

The mode of entry will also be dependent upon the nature of the business. For example, manufacturing industries will, in many cases, establish a physical presence in the market in which they wish to operate. The aerospace industry is an exception, since the final product is capable of moving itself to the chosen market. In the case of service industries the distinction can be made between hard and soft services (Blomstermo and Deo Sharma, 2005). Hard services are those in which production and consumption can be decoupled, such as software or design services where the

Figure 6.1 Market and entry mode selection model

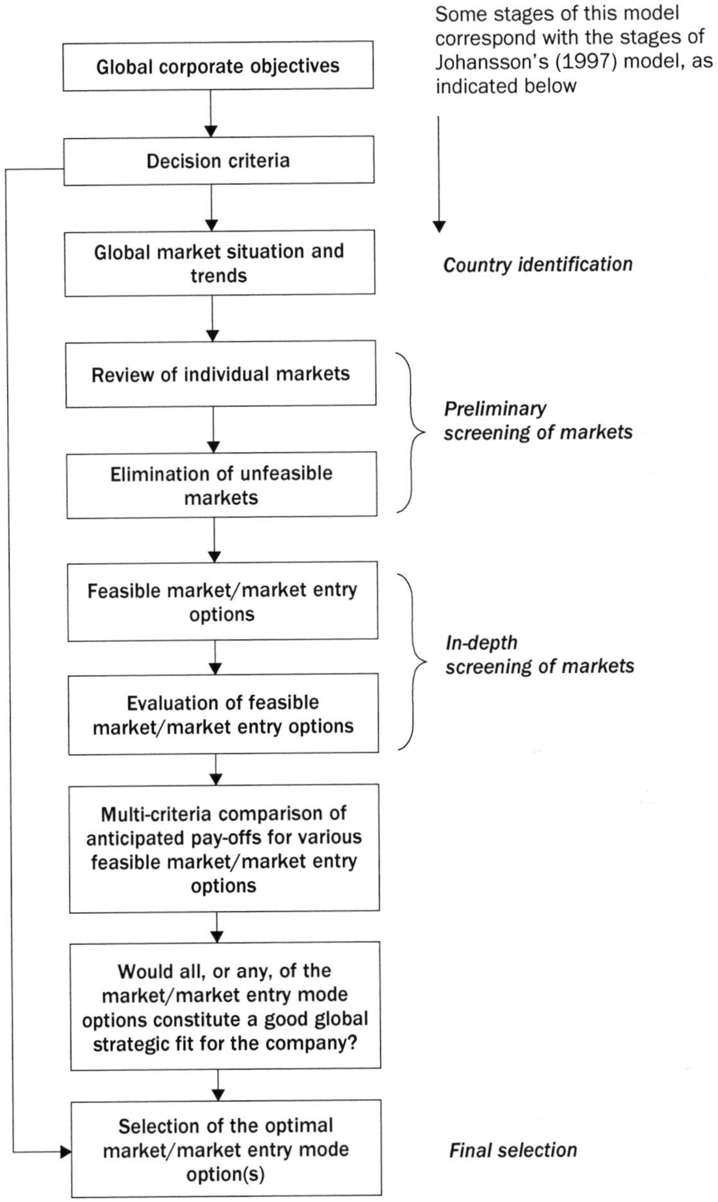

Some stages of this model correspond with the stages of Johansson's (1997) model, as indicated below

```
┌─────────────────────────────┐
│ Global corporate objectives │
└─────────────────────────────┘
              │
              ▼
┌─────────────────────────────┐
│      Decision criteria      │
└─────────────────────────────┘
              │
              ▼
┌─────────────────────────────┐
│ Global market situation and │      *Country identification*
│           trends            │
└─────────────────────────────┘
              │
              ▼
┌─────────────────────────────┐
│ Review of individual markets│
└─────────────────────────────┘      *Preliminary
              │                        screening of markets*
              ▼
┌─────────────────────────────┐
│  Elimination of unfeasible  │
│           markets           │
└─────────────────────────────┘
              │
              ▼
┌─────────────────────────────┐
│ Feasible market/market entry│
│           options           │
└─────────────────────────────┘      *In-depth
              │                        screening of markets*
              ▼
┌─────────────────────────────┐
│    Evaluation of feasible   │
│ market/market entry options │
└─────────────────────────────┘
              │
              ▼
┌─────────────────────────────┐
│  Multi-criteria comparison of│
│ anticipated pay-offs for various│
│ feasible market/market entry│
│           options           │
└─────────────────────────────┘
              │
              ▼
┌─────────────────────────────┐
│   Would all, or any, of the │
│   market/market entry mode  │
│ options constitute a good global│
│ strategic fit for the company?│
└─────────────────────────────┘
              │
              ▼
┌─────────────────────────────┐
│   Selection of the optimal  │
│ market/market entry mode    │      *Final selection*
│         option(s)           │
└─────────────────────────────┘
```

Source: adapted from Koch (2001); Johansson (1997)

output can be transferred electronically. Such services can often be standardised, making mass production feasible. By contrast, with soft services production and consumption occur at the same point in time and location. The service provider, or its representative, must be physically present in the target market from day one of operations. The suppliers are an integral part of the service (Palmer and Cole, 1995), and higher control is needed over the production process. Hotels and hospitals are a case in point. The quality of the interaction experience of customers with the firm is an important determinant of continuing business and repeat purchases. It has been argued that management consultancy is a soft service, but to a large extent it has become a hybrid, where there are some customer-facing agents but often a large number of 'back-office' staff.

From the perspective of the target country, the government will want to encourage FDI and a physical operation set up in the country so that the local economy will benefit, the national economy will benefit if the product is exported and any available technology can be transferred. The government will try to develop clusters of expertise so that a snowball effect will attract further companies in similar or related industries into the region. Notable examples of the cluster effect are software outsourcing in Bangalore and the high-tech area of Silicon Valley. The development of Silicon Valley is typical of a cluster. Initially, when a number of computer technology companies started in the area, they needed finance, and venture capitalists started to open offices around them. As the high-tech companies became successful their suppliers also opened offices and factories close by. As the industry grew it made sense for computer engineers to move to the area, because the job prospects were better with such a concentration of employers. These initiatives are obviously important since, in a survey in 2005, more than 1,400 organisations were identified as being involved in the promotion of clusters (UNCTAD, 2007). Apart from lobbying policy-makers, these organisations are involved in supply-chain development, training, joint R&D projects, marketing of the region and attracting foreign direct investment.

In the Middle East, which is currently benefiting from high oil prices, governments are investing their income to reduce their dependence upon future oil revenues. The economies are being developed by a well-educated business class and powered by a relatively young population seeking lasting prosperity. Dubai has established internet and media cities, installing high-speed data transmission networks in office parks, and is actively attracting small businesses to the industry cluster. Additionally, Hewlett-Packard, Microsoft and Cisco Systems have all opened offices there, with a representative of Cisco Systems describing the area as a 'mini Silicon Valley'. The Middle East currently represents Cisco's fastest-growing region due to local telecommunications deregulation and the increasing sophistication of local businesses that are leapfrogging European and US firms by buying the latest video-streaming and data services. A government official said that the priorities are healthcare, education and diversification away from an oil-and-gas-based economy. At the same time Dubai has established a stock exchange, the Dubai International Financial Exchange, and has attracted major banks to handle the large number of initial public offerings (IPOs) that will fund this growth and help liberalise the market, encouraging wider ownership of the new companies.

Similarly, Saudi Arabia has established the new $27 billion King Abdullah Economic City on the banks of the Red Sea, with the intention that this will be a giant port with manufacturing businesses, particularly petrochemicals.

Thirty per cent of the project equity will be offered to investors on the stock exchange. A further example of a country seeing its economy boosted by the arrival of foreign firms is Russia, where growth in the domestic economy is being fuelled by the arrival of multinational retailers which have established bases in the country. In 2005 Russia attracted $16.7 billion of FDI, with Coca-Cola acquiring a fruit-juice maker, Heineken acquiring local brewers and both Toyota and Volkswagen establishing automobile factories. Other companies establishing factories include Carlsberg, Nestlé and Whirlpool, the domestic appliance manufacturer, in partnership with the Turkish Vestel Group. By 2007 FDI reached its highest peak in the first half of the year, at a little less than $25 billion (Pavlotsky, 2007).

Current conventional wisdom also suggests that US multinationals are moving cutting-edge R&D to China in order to take advantage of vast legions of low-cost technologically skilled workers. However, the real extent of innovative activity performed in China by US multinationals is quite modest. In 2004 US firms spent $622 million on R&D in China; an amount that was about 0.3 per cent of the total R&D undertaken globally by these firms. China accounted for less than 13 per cent of total R&D undertaken by US firms within the Asian region. It is hard to reconcile these small numbers with the view that US firms are shifting the locus of their R&D activities to China. US FDI in China is surprisingly small relative to nearly any relevant benchmark. US firms account for a small component of total FDI inflows into China. US affiliates have contributed very little to Chinese fixed-asset investment or employment growth. Moreover, in 2004 the Chinese operations of US firms accounted for only 1.9 per cent of total foreign affiliate sales and 0.7 per cent of total foreign affiliate assets. US CEOs like Intel's Craig Barrett have publicly asserted that China poses a threat to the current dominance of US-based technology firms, including his own. More academic analyses suggest that China is rapidly becoming an important global centre of innovation. In its 2005 annual survey of global FDI trends, the *World Investment Report* singled out the growth of foreign R&D centres in China, then numbering several hundred, as a development of particular significance (UNCTAD, 2005). Other scholars, including Schott (2007) and Rodrik (2006), have found an unusually high degree of technological sophistication in China's export pattern, driven by the country's own technological base.

Foreign investment in the service sector is expected to maintain robust growth, as the service industry will be further opened up to foreign investors while investment in manufacturing is likely to decrease. Foreign investors largely relied on 'greenfield' projects when investing in China, but the country saw more and more mergers and acquisitions by foreign investors in the first half of 2007. Annual FDI in China has remained flat at around US$60 billion in recent years. The Ministry of Commerce approved 18,683 foreign-invested enterprises in the first six months of 2007, down 5.4 per cent from the previous year. China is now encouraging investments in high-value-added manufacturing sectors and service industries while turning down foreign investments in high-pollution and low-efficiency ventures (*People's Daily Online*, 2007b).

It was reported that FDI in India during 2006 would double, as Kamal Nath, India's minister of commerce and industry, said inflows were expected to surpass $11 billion in 2006–2007, compared with $5.5 billion the previous year (Yee, 2006). In fact, they reached $12.9 billion.[2] 'There have been huge investments coming in the software industry, financial services and manufacturing,' said Mr Nath. The largest growth in FDI was in telecoms, energy, services, electrical equipment and transportation, due to loosening government policies and simplification of policies and procedures. While India has increased allowed FDI levels in sectors such as telecoms to 74 per cent, investment in other sectors remains capped below 50 per cent or is entirely restricted. Retail is a point of contention for multibrand international chains such as Wal-Mart and Tesco, which must seek Indian partners to enter the fast-growing Indian market. Single-brand retailers such as Nike and Benetton are limited to 49 per cent FDI. Behind mainland China, Hong Kong and Singapore were the second- and third-largest recipients of FDI in the Asia region in 2005, attracting $36 billion and $20 billion respectively, according to UNCTAD (2005). Other members of the Association of South-East Asian Nations (ASEAN) experienced their highest growth in FDI inflows. Indonesia, for example, attracted $5.3 billion.

With the developing nations, the direction of FDI is not all one way. In 2006 alone, Brazilian multinationals invested abroad more than the country received as FDI, to the extent that Brazilian multinationals currently have a total amount of investment abroad of over US$106 billion. From January to November 2006, Brazilian multinationals made FDI overseas of approximately US$25 billion (*O Globo*, 2007). China's investment overseas registered annual growth of 60 per cent over the five years to 2006: by the end of 2006 its direct investment abroad reached $90.6 billion, covering 172 nations and regions. Despite the strong growth, China's outgoing FDI still remains weak, especially in comparison to the huge inflow of overseas capital.[3] Much of China's investment abroad has been by acquisition, particularly in energy and primary resources as it secures supplies for its economic growth.

The Central Bank of India proposed to increase outward investment to control liquidity and rein in the rupee. It suggested that further liberalisation of norms would increase outflow of funds and help to control the liquidity position, but the fact is that India's investment abroad is already increasing rapidly. The total international assets of India have increased at an annual compound rate of 24.2 per cent, against 12.6 per cent annual rise in total international liabilities, between 2001–2002 and 2006–2007. In fact, the outflow under direct investment stagnated during the early part of the current decade, but in the last two years after liberalisation of norms for outward investment it has grown rapidly. Much of India's investment overseas has been by acquisition.

Translating strategy into action

For many CEOs strategy execution is far more difficult than strategy creation. Research has shown that over 90 per cent of formulated strategies in the UK and USA failed to be completed on time and deliver the expected outcomes (McManus and Botten, 2006). Lou Gerstner commented at IBM that while the thinking was good the execution was poor, and similarly at Xerox the stock was downgraded when market analysts perceived a problem with execution of the firm's excellent plans (Garr, 2000). It would appear that the general management of a firm and its ability to implement strategies well are a significant source of competitive advantage.

All strategy involves a significant level of change: this is particularly true when the chosen strategy involves acquisition or merger in the pursuit of synergies and operating efficiencies. There are a number of challenges inherent in the choice of structure that a firm must overcome. Each potential structure will have associated costs and benefits. A greater number of divisions and geographical locations will usually be more expensive, but if it increases local responsiveness in a soft service industry the benefits should outweigh the costs. Process specialisation, i.e. functional structures, in an organisation will be appropriate where products are standardised, there are high volumes and economies of scale are available. Where the focus is around customers, products or markets and there is a greater emphasis on purpose, a structure involving SBUs is more appropriate.

There will need to be an appropriate balance struck between the conflicting demands of centralisation and autonomy. Taking the example of soft services again, how much autonomy must a subsidiary be given to ensure that local market perceptions and attitudes are ideal? Within the same set-up, how big should the corporate centre be and what should be its role? The parenting skills will be important whether the firm is centralised or decentralised. Organisations need to look carefully at the corporate centre and decide where it can add value. This may well be through acting as a centre of excellence taking responsibility for transferring best practice throughout the organisation and for overall strategic planning. The chosen structure must achieve the twin goals of coordination and communication across the various parts of the business, both horizontally between subsidiaries and vertically between the corporate centre and the subsidiaries themselves.

Asea Brown Boveri (ABB), which competes in over 60 different markets and consists of more than 1,300 subsidiary companies, faces a difficult task of integration across its organisation. This has been accomplished by heavy investment in its Abacus IT system, global managers and a worldwide matrix organisation (Simons, 1992). Contrast this with Royal Dutch Shell, where the reporting of overstatement of the firm's oil reserves was claimed to be due to the existence of two distinctly separate but equal holding companies (Cummins et al., 2004). Over time different reporting practices had become embedded, and divisions were even allowed to use and interpret geological data in different ways. Shortly afterwards the firm went through the process of integration into one reporting structure, but not before some embarrassing press conferences and analysts' meetings.

Business integration and strategy

The structure within a business unit will be dependent upon the competitive situation with which it is faced. It may be that there will be different business structures within the overall organisation. To some extent the issues to be raised here are the same as those discussed for corporate structure. The structure chosen must facilitate the flow of information around the business unit and out to other parts of the organisation. The creation of 'silos' of information and knowledge within a division of the firm, and the conflicts that ensue, can only act against the successful implementation of the firm's strategy. The example of McKinsey, the consulting firm, shows the importance of knowledge transfer. Working with a variety of clients across the globe, continued effectiveness can only be achieved by sharing knowledge and previously developed processes between the different offices and groups which make up the organisation. Managing across specialisms and industry groups is essential to the successful implementation of McKinsey's overall strategy (Berhin, 2005).

Decisions need to be committed to by the people responsible for their execution, who will be required to subordinate their own goals to those of the organisation. A method of ensuring goal congruence is required which will provide feedback on the correct things that need to be accomplished in the strategy execution process. Feedback is essential to organisational change and/or adaptation at all levels. CEOs need to know that things are 'on course' or close to it, bearing in mind the comments about emergent strategy, and others in the organisation need to know that they are doing the right things well enough to hit targets. It is unlikely that senior management will get everything perfectly right at the first attempt, but the control measures taken should facilitate fine-tuning of plans and implementation processes in a timely fashion. Even good incentives do not create motivation, but they will guide it in the correct direction and strengthen it. At the end of the day, effective motivation can balance the outcome between the possible and the impossible.

With greater emphasis on knowledge management and knowledge sharing, there are problems in defining the measures to be used to recognise good behaviour. Knowledge sharing usually involves a change from 'look up and yell down' modes of management to horizontal knowledge-sharing behaviours: it is important that the value of knowledge sharing be reflected in the ongoing personnel evaluation, periodic merit review or pay bonuses of the organisation, so that managers and staff can see that knowledge sharing is one of the principal behaviours that the organisation encourages and rewards. It is important that knowledge sharing be designated as one of a small number of core behaviours that are rewarded in the performance review system. Getting agreement across any large organisation to focus on knowledge sharing is not easy, and even when accomplished does not have any instant effect. In the short run there is often cynicism and posturing, but the experience of organisations, particularly large consulting firms, is that over time such a change sends an unmistakable signal throughout the organisation which does accelerate the intended behavioural change. Jack Welch (2005: 47) notes:

> differentiation rewards those members of the team who deserve it. By the way, that annoys only the underperformers. To everyone else, it seems fair. And a fair environment promotes teamwork. Better yet, it motivates people to give their all, and that's what you want.

While formal motivation incentives are important for the long-run sustainability of a knowledge-management programme, it is easy to overestimate their value. The absence of formal incentives in the early days of knowledge sharing can become a pretext for not implementing a programme. The establishment of rewards for individual knowledge-sharing activities can signal the importance of knowledge sharing, but also runs the risk of creating expectations of rewards for behaviour that should be part of the normal way of conducting the business of the organisation.

In the long term, however, the establishment of motivation through the reward system of the organisation should create a clear value framework which confirms that knowledge sharing is part of the permanent fabric of the organisation. If you are doing it right, your future, while not completely guaranteed, is certainly more sustainable.

Key chapter messages

- Successful firms are those that have the vision and courage to challenge existing business models and develop innovative ways to bring value to the market more efficiently and effectively than the competition.

- Vision must be a compelling story that all departments and levels of an organisation can accept and believe to be achievable.

- The strategy that an organisation follows emerges from a number of drivers.

- The clarity of the strategies devised will make the implementation process that much easier. A good strategy does not necessarily make for a good outcome, but a poor strategy will always lead to a poor outcome.

- In many industries the ubiquity of modern communications and the increasing rapidity of transport systems have caused a convergence of tastes and preferences of consumers in an increasing number of nations.

- For a market that is already globally concentrated, market entry may be purely defensive to focus a competitor's attention on its home market and limit its willingness to expand further overseas.

- In strategic terms the level of resource commitment will be dependent upon both high demand and relatively high certainty about that demand.

- The quality of the interaction experience of a firm's customers is an important determinant of continuing business and repeat purchases.

- Conventional wisdom suggests that many multinationals are moving cutting-edge R&D to other nation-states, such as China, in order to take advantage of vast legions of low-cost technologically skilled workers.

- The establishment of rewards for individual knowledge-sharing activities can signal the importance of knowledge sharing, but also runs the risk of creating expectations of rewards for behaviour that should be part of the normal way of conducting the business of the organisation.

Notes

1. See www.airdeccan.net.
2. See http://dipp.nic.in/fdi_statistics/india_fdi_index.htm.
3. See www.china.org.cn/english/business/232205.htm.

7

Case study: China, India and Russia – a strategic and market perspective within the global software industry

Introduction

The last decade has witnessed the emergence of China and India as the two most significant economies in the global competitive landscape. Their prominence is due not only to rapidly growing local markets but also to a phenomenally increasing concentration of economic and innovative activities taking place in these two countries. Particularly in the context of the global software industry, India has acquired the reputation of a leading 'software nation', while China is fast gaining ground and emerging as a serious player. Various economic indicators, including the flow of FDI, testify to the significance of India and China in the global software industry landscape.

Interestingly, however, the evolution and growth trajectories of the Chinese software industry differ considerably from those of the Indian industry. And the situation in both countries differs considerably from that in Russia: although considered as an 'emerging' market, the software industry in Russia is in fact a far more mature industry than is the case in the Asian nations.

This case study provides a comparative analysis of the markets and dynamics of the Chinese, Indian and Russian software industries, and discusses implications for the global industry. Specifically, employing a strategic management perspective, the case presents competitive assessments of the software industries in the three countries, explores their interrelationships and discusses their competitive positioning strategies. In doing so, it presents an analysis of the segmentation within the global software industry and discusses customer-oriented and market-oriented strategies for each country. Finally, in view of the strengthening foothold of China, India and Russia, the case concludes by discussing implications for the global software industry.

Market segmentation

According to Professor Michael Porter (1986), industry segmentation is the division of an industry into sections for the purposes of developing competitive strategy. Industry segmentation combines customer purchasing behaviour (market segmentation) with the behaviour of costs – both production costs and the costs of serving different customers. Segmentation encompasses the entire value chain. It exposes the differences in structural attractiveness among segments and the conflicts in serving many segments simultaneously. In essence, segmentation is a division of an industry into subsidiary units whereby such units can be analysed for the purpose of developing competitive strategies.

The fundamental dynamics of the software industry are characterised by firms engaged in software research and development and the provision of products and services. Classical theory on market segmentation initially explained it as a marketing strategy that firms choose to adopt. The concept of market segmentation was defined as viewing a heterogeneous market (one characterised by divergent demand) as a number of smaller homogeneous markets in response to differing product preferences among important market segments. The goal of market segmentation is to describe such within-product category conditions that point to valued attributes and benefits (Figure 7.1).

Market segmentation has been the software industry's practical approach to finding a mechanism for the task of meeting consumers' wants and needs. Consider what is at issue. Regarding any one offering, management has resources to invest in responding to a finite set of consumer wants. Within a product category, it considers the diverse nature of wants, the current state of want satisfaction – reflecting its own and competitive responses – and its likely ability to obtain a satisfactory return from supporting or continuing to support the offering. Providing information about consumer wants within a market is the task of market segmentation analysis.

Market segmentation allows firms which operate at a global level to differentiate clusters of added value. Russia,

Figure 7.1 Market segmentation of the global software industry

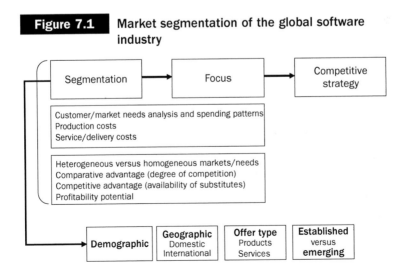

China and India compete within a global industry, and as such rely on close collaborations with partner organisations. Increasing competitiveness within market sectors requires individual firms to position their resources where they can best leverage added value and shareholder returns. For both existing firms and new firms entering the software market, making decisions on how to position themselves and become competitive in a global market is important.

Competitive scope

Segmentation is necessary to address the central question of competitive scope within an industry, or what segments of an industry a firm should serve and how it should serve them. It is also the basis for the choice of focus strategies, since it exposes segments that are poorly served by broadly targeted competitors in which focus can be both sustainable and profitable. Broadly targeted competitors must also understand industry segmentation, because it reveals areas where they are vulnerable to focusers and may suggest unattractive segments that are best left to competitors. Attention to segmentation from a strategic perspective is increasingly important because new developments in technology are altering some of the old rules of segmentation, with implications for both focusers and broadly targeted firms. The question here is 'In which parts of the industry can the firm expect the highest long-term returns?' In practical terms, within which market segments will it be possible for the firm to:

- develop a supportable advantage relative to competitors in other, possibly neighbouring, segments?
- dispute competitors' attractive returns on any investments required to enter the chosen segments?

The most important attribute of a strategic market segment is its defensibility. Evidence that a segment exists is the barriers to competition that surround it. The nature of market segmentation involves firms designing products and services that satisfy smaller homogeneous groups within the total market. Once these groups have been identified, and their needs understood, the firm may be able to develop a market mix appropriate for servicing a subgroup it considers a potential and profitable market. It could be argued, however, that as we head towards the year 2010 firms should stop thinking of customers as part of a homogeneous market, and should consider instead customers as distinct units, each requiring its own unique strategies in product policy, promotional strategy, pricing, distribution methods and direct-selling techniques (i.e. the 'everybody' markets – the philosophy of maximising the value of contact with each customer). Evidence would suggest that future market strategies will need to be directed towards constantly changing market needs. Under such conditions market awareness, organisational flexibility, strategic vision and external relationships are important strategic capabilities. Getting closer to the customer requires assessment of the customer's needs and wants. The purpose of this assessment is to find an actual or potential competitive advantage.

Strategies and interrelationships

Academics such as Michael Porter have applied their ideas on interrelationships and horizontal strategies to the analysis of corporate strategy. The major issue seems to be how to leverage the synergy across different value chains in the hope of making the total value of the diversified company higher than the summation of individual businesses' values as they stand alone. According to Porter (1986), interrelationships are not the fuzzy notions of fit, but tangible opportunities to reduce costs or enhance differentiation in virtually any activity in the value chain. There are three types of interrelationships: tangible, intangible and competitor. While tangible interrelationships arise from opportunities to share activities in the value chain, intangible interrelationships involve the transfer of management know-how among separate value chains, and competitor interrelationships stem from the existence of rivals which actually or potentially compete with the firm in more than one business unit.

Porter (ibid.) uses similar reasoning in exploring the issues of globalisation and firms' competition across borders. Firms considering internationalisation must take care of the issue of how they can leverage the competitive advantage in their home countries and extend it into the global arena, i.e. take advantage of synergies across locations. As a first step, it is important to understand the differences between a multidomestic and a global industry. In multidomestic industries, competition in each country (or small groups of countries) is essentially independent of competition in other countries. The definition of a global industry is an industry in which a firm's competitive position in one country is significantly affected by its position in other countries, or vice versa. The implications of competitive strategies are quite different for a multidomestic and a global industry. In a multidomestic industry, the firm's international strategy should be 'country-centred': international strategy collapses to a series of domestic strategies. In a global industry, a firm must in some way integrate its activities on a worldwide basis to capture the linkages between countries. The integration will require more than transferring intangible assets among countries, though it will include such transfers. All of the important competitors in global industries compete worldwide with increasingly coordinated strategies.

Given the characteristics of the software industry and the current positioning of BRIC software firms, will internationalisation require global strategies or multiregional strategies? For example, to what extent can Indian firms leverage their success in the outsourcing business in the US market and extend it to other countries and regions? Many Chinese software firms which have successfully won Japanese outsourcing contracts have the ambitious goal of extending their success into the US and European markets and competing with the incumbent Indian firms in these markets. Whether these types of hopes can become a reality to a large extent depends on the firms correctly understanding this issue and thus adopting the right mix of strategies. Here we should consider the market segments of the software industry. Some segments of the industry, such as packaged software, are global, but others, such as consulting services, are multidomestic.

The software industry: a Chinese perspective

Firms entering the software industry often begin by competing on wage structuring (cost differentiation). This allows firms to sell services that focus on the low end of the value chain – this may include such activities as software coding. As firms develop domain expertise they move up the value chain and attract investment funds, which allows them to develop market niches and attract FDI funding. Moving into niches is as much a first-mover as a late-entrant market strategy, and can bring many of the benefits of being first.

China's technology policy through the early 1990s favoured the large state-owned enterprises (SOEs) and government research institutes, following the model of Japan and Korea.

However, most Chinese ministers lacked understanding of both the technologies they sought to develop and the needs of Chinese industry, and Chinese SOEs and research institutes were unable to abandon the practices and structures of the planned economy. China also faced a different international environment than Korea and Japan a decade or so earlier – one which was characterised by an accelerating pace of innovation and intensifying global competition. As a result, the strategies of the 1980s and early 1990s produced very little success.

Two decades of change in China's science and technology system have been both disruptive and remarkable at the same time. The Chinese economy is stronger today than most would have predicted in the 1980s, with impressive achievements in building a national telecommunications infrastructure and widespread adoption of IT, particularly wireless phones and related telecommunications products. The new technology regime has been extremely successful in the development of IT manufacturing capabilities, where relationships between domestic firms and foreign investors – particularly from Taiwan and Hong Kong – have contributed to rapid development of the domestic capacity for low-cost manufacture of computers, consumer electronics and communications equipment. While initially these ventures were restricted to lower-technology, labour-intensive processes, over time their technical capabilities have increased. China is now manufacturing laptop computers and sophisticated electronic components for export. In 2002 China was the third-largest IT manufacturing centre in the world, following only the USA and Japan.

There are about 20 million small to medium-sized enterprises in China. In 2004 there were approximately 10,000 registered software firms employing around 600,000 people providing products and services in packaged software, financial services, security systems, electronic publishing and educational and health-related products.

Domestic Chinese software firms are typically characterised by the entrepreneur class focused on niche markets that lack economy of scale. There is some clustering of software firms. Zhongguancuan Science and Technology Park in Beijing represents China's Silicon Valley and is home to Oracle, IBM and Microsoft subsidiaries as well as dozens of other software firms. Beijing is by far the largest software-producing district, with a balanced industry including packaged, industrial and security software as well as export. Beijing's prominence is in part due to it being a centre for government and leading educational and research institutions.

As of 2005 only a handful of firms have more than 1,000 employees or sales revenues in excess $90 million. Foreign corporations, including Oracle, IBM and Microsoft, dominate the software product market in China. According to CCID Consulting in Beijing, the packaged software industry in China reached $1.3 billion in sales, which provided 37,000 jobs and generated £220 million in tax revenue (McManus et al., 2007a). The top five software vendors accounted for 20 per cent of sales. In recent years the internal Chinese market has seen a large number of new vendors; for example, the market for enterprise resource management software has increased tenfold in the last five years. Although dominated by its domestic market strategy, the Chinese software industry is moving forward on many fronts – today software services, primarily systems integration, account for more than half of China's total software output.

The importance of vision in international markets cannot be overestimated. The most successful software firms (and exporters) have implemented their visions and sustained lead market positions in products and services. Markets are composed of many consumers, but consumers alone do not make a market. Markets require not only purchasers and a willingness to buy; they also need purchasing power and the authority to buy. Bringing products and services to international markets is an established activity for many Western firms. The changing landscape, however, with the composition of international markets and the emergence of new entrants and organisational forms, is creating new pressures for the emerging economies.

Some Chinese firms have managed to establish strong international brands, largely through partnerships – for example, US firm Computer Associates partnered with Neusoft Group, a software company based in Shenyang in north-east China. The partnership aims to develop new-generation industrial solutions to serve Chinese customers better.

The deepening of technological or other forms of capability is one way in which stronger Chinese firms differentiate themselves from their weaker rivals. For example, UFSoft and Kingdee are the only software firms ranked in the top ten PSVs in China. As previously stated, there are a considerable number of firms that compete on cost alone, and although cost advantage is attractive to some consumers it may be a weakness when operating in the global marketplace. The more enlightened Chinese firms have attempted to move up the technological value chain, so as not to compete with the many smaller firms which cannot function at that level, but again this has its drawbacks: with the shortage of skilled professional software engineers, the majority of Chinese companies are struggling to make their presence felt in many international markets.

The software industry: an Indian perspective

Perhaps the most striking contrast with the Chinese software industry is India's strategic success in earning export revenues and research and development income. Given the relative population sizes of each country, one might have expected that the gulf between the two would have narrowed in time; but, although the strategies have converged to some degree, the cultural differences have not (Figure 7.2).

As a result of the technological fixation on software engineering and the emphasis on cultural content of software as opposed to pure function, India has used its knowledge of Western business culture and its vast English-speaking population to enhance its market presence in many areas of product engineering and software services provision. This strategy culminated in advances in software engineering which were transferred into high-value software products. India's offshore capability has allowed it to take advantage of Western technology and innovations in software research and development. Evidence would suggest that while many large Western firms are moving their operations overseas, many of the offshore Indian software houses are pursuing aggressive and targeted strategies to expand their product and service market capabilities. Indian

Figure 7.2 China and India: comparative analysis of strengths and weaknesses

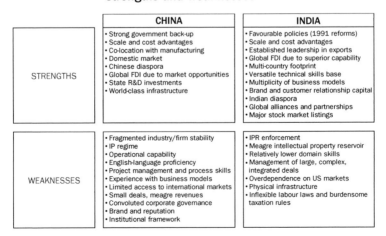

	CHINA	INDIA
STRENGTHS	• Strong government back-up • Scale and cost advantages • Co-location with manufacturing • Domestic market • Chinese diaspora • Global FDI due to market opportunities • State R&D investments • World-class infrastructure	• Favourable policies (1991 reforms) • Scale and cost advantages • Established leadership in exports • Global FDI due to superior capability • Multi-country footprint • Versatile technical skills base • Multiplicity of business models • Brand and customer relationship capital • Indian diaspora • Global alliances and partnerships • Major stock market listings
WEAKNESSES	• Fragmented industry/firm stability • IP regime • Operational capability • English-language proficiency • Project management and process skills • Experience with business models • Limited access to international markets • Small deals, meagre revenues • Convoluted corporate governance • Brand and reputation • Institutional framework	• IPR enforcement • Meagre intellectual property reservoir • Relatively lower domain skills • Management of large, complex, integrated deals • Overdependence on US markets • Physical infrastructure • Inflexible labour laws and burdensome taxation rules

firms want to be more than low-cost vendors: they want to be leaders in innovation. This may seem a bit ambitious, but it is telling that Infosys and Wipro, two of the most successful Indian software firms, aim to provide software development services to US firms by developing their own products. Ranjit Singh, a key figure in Xerox's internet software development, advanced an explanation of this happening when he said that 'the limits of the arbitrage model that exploits offshore are being reached'.[1]

From its early origins in the mid-1980s as a contract service provider to the USA and Europe, India has been very successful in establishing a major domestic computer software and export services industry. But for many years the India software industry was considered a fringe provider by most multinational firms.

India's software firms are clustered around the big cities of Bangalore, Hyderabad, Mumbai (previously Bombay), Pune, Delhi (India's capital, in the north), Chennai (previously Madras) and Calcutta. Bangalore is by far the most vibrant of all software cities in India and is often referred to as India's 'Silicon Valley' (Sharma, 1994). There are varying accounts of how many software firms are actually located in Bangalore because of differing definitions of what constitutes software development. Altogether it is estimated that there are about 220 software firms in Bangalore, the majority of which are medium-sized, i.e. between 100 and 150 employees; only about 10 per cent have over 500 employees. More than two-thirds of the companies in Bangalore are Indian. There is also a wide range of software activities, from the basic body-shopping activities to cutting-edge research. Bangalore has emerged quickly as a software centre, surpassing Mumbai, one of the first software centres in India. Firms in Bangalore were among the first in India to react to the PC revolution. There is therefore a feeling that, on the whole, the activities undertaken by the more established firms and the multinationals in Bangalore are more sophisticated and high-tech than those in other Indian cities.

Lack of earnings in India's domestic markets has forced many software firms to seek growth by moving into international export markets, mostly concentrated in the USA and Europe. In terms of products and services, there have been continuous exports of software products since the early 1990s. Such products include enterprise systems and database tools; however, these product-based exports even today represent only a small proportion of India's export capability. In essence, India is still led by exporting services.

For India the nature of demand has been critical. With a constant flow of new entrants to the software industry, profits from the sale of traditional services are likely to fall in the future; revenue growth will depend only on growth in numbers of software workers. In order to survive the increased level of competition in the world market, Indian firms would have to develop new products that are at the high end of the value chain. In this context, while India's largest software service firms, Tata, Wipro and Infosys, reported significant increases in profits in the last few years, they have experienced increasing competition from a number of low-cost Asian nations such as Vietnam. India also faces challenges within its labour markets – historically there has been a high premium placed on talent without a sense of ownership, which has led to a high attrition rate among software professionals; this in turn has led to restricted scope and chances for growth in high-value market sectors like telecommunications and infrastructure services.

Evidence would suggest that many large Indian firms are developing expertise in the so-called vertical domain areas because they offer a rise up the value chain into areas of work that are longer term and more lucrative than traditional development tasks. In addition, aggressive attempts have been made by a small number of Indian companies to globalise through acquisition, by setting up overseas development sites or acquiring a 'front-end' marketing capability. One challenge of acquisition is managing the process of absorption. This is a useful cultural test for Indian companies, whose takeovers and mergers have typically been confined to targets owned by fellow Indians, albeit living in the USA.

Russia's software industry

Although Russia is abundant in natural resources (such as oil, gas and coal), its economic performance was weak for much of the 1990s due to the country's poor macroeconomic strategy, its structural economic weaknesses and the lack of political and institutional support for business. In 2000 a new economic programme was introduced based on free-market principles and calling for the extension of equal opportunities to all economic actors, the guarantee of property rights and the elimination of bureaucratic constraints on business (World Bank, 2004). Further reforms in Russia's taxation, budgetary, legal and corporate governance systems and labour laws have since been introduced, and Russia is now enjoying an economic renaissance. Although levels of domestic and foreign direct investment remain low and are a future challenge to the Russian economy, a recent report by Goldman Sachs (2003) suggests Russia could be one of the six top economies in the world by 2050.

The Russian software industry has its roots in space research and defence. During the 1950s Russia's focus was principally in software engineering and engineering research; during the 1960s and 1970s it concentrated on providing programming capability to its national defence suppliers. Although Russia had developed world-class capabilities in both industrial software development and computer science research, its expertise was generally not for sale outside the Eastern bloc. This persisted until the early 1990s, when the introduction of *perestroika* was the catalyst for free-market reform. Private firms formed to provide systems integration and software services for the emerging domestic and international markets.

Russia demonstrates one of the best growth rates in computer sales. Firms such as the Moscow-based Luxoft, with 1,600 employees and $45 million in sales, emerged to take advantage of the new markets; estimated total sales of Russian software houses in 2005 were $1 billion. Even though figures vary, the share of the software services market belonging to Russian and Eastern European companies is likely to increase from 5 to 8 per cent over the next two years, fuelled by the growing global demand for high-quality software engineering capability and cost differentials (McManus et al., 2007a). Although Russia has abundant software engineering capability and a highly educated workforce (in a typical Russian software firm 15 per cent of workers have PhDs), its market conditions are complex and capable of rapid change, leading to commercial risks as well as opportunities for new market entrants (Bridgewater, 2000). Commercial risk and concerns about Russia's future political stability are making global investors oversensitive – thus the Russian government will have to do more to offset these commercial risks.

Russian software firms fall into two categories: Russian-owned companies (such as the IBS Group and Luxoft), and Western-owned firms with branches in Russia (for example, Sun Microsystems in Moscow). Established

Russian software houses were founded from the old Soviet institutions and in many instances dominate the domestic markets. In the early days product and market development was financed by the businesses themselves and the products found their way to the market without access to banks and venture capital. Like all domestic Chinese software firms, Russian software-house customers are large companies in the leading industries, such as banking and gas and oil production. The expansion and growth of offshore development have helped the Russian software industry gain a foothold in the international market. Over the years 2000–2002, during a time of severe recession in the markets of developed countries, the outsourcing industry in Russia gathered strength and momentum, doubling its export turnover to $350 million by 2002. Technical and business solutions as well as hi-tech services offered by Russian software companies have become invaluable tools for many leading companies worldwide. For a few Russian firms outsourcing has provided the means to acquire business and market knowledge. To compete with Indian software firms, some market observers believe Russian firms will need to generate an additional $200 million in annual revenues.

The attractiveness of international software development markets has prompted firms to pool their ideas and strategies to overcome the obstacles to market entry. Clusters of firms around St Petersburg, close to the Finnish, Swedish and North European borders, have a geographical advantage for offshoring development, and a practically non-existent internal market. With dozens of firms employing from 50 to 250 people, this is one of the most vibrant offshore development centres in Russia (Terekhov, 2001).

The key in part to Russia's future success lies in the reshaping of its industry to compete with the industry élites. In 2001 Russia signed the Okinawa Charter, which stresses the importance of computer technologies for the development of a modern information society. Russia's move to a free-market economy and its increasing political stability make it an attractive proposition for Western investors. Its well-educated workforce and technical strengths in science research and development should allow Russian to gain an increasing share of the global software market. Previous inadequacies such as the legislative framework, including laws governing intellectual property, software export and taxation, as well as ongoing enforcement still require attention, as do business bureaucracy and corruption.

Escalating development costs in the West have created increasing value consciousness on the part of chief executives, motivating them to search for price-competitive nations which have the skills and ability to deliver high-quality products. In this respect Russia is seen to have a distinct competitive advantage over China and India. Domestically, Russian consumer tastes are becoming more sophisticated and product-based technology is in high demand. This consumer-led push demand has aided and strengthened the Russian domestic software industry, allowing SMEs and individual entrepreneurs to set up businesses in urban centres such as Moscow and St Petersburg.

Conclusions: some implications for the industry

India, Russia and China have made strategic inroads, but there is a long way to go before world-class software industry clusters emerge in their economies. India's main challenge is to go beyond the success of software services exports and strengthen its weakest link in the sector: hardware development and manufacturing. China has been strong in the hardware sector but lags far behind India in the software sector, especially in exports. Russia's highly developed infrastructure and economic and technological strengths will help to improve its market position in software services. Its main challenge is maintaining a cost basis that is competitive to those of China and India. All three countries face the difficult task of building on their strengths, extending them into other sectors and fostering innovation capability in order to move up the value chain in the world market. With the rapid growth of the two most populous economies in the world, there will be explosive domestic demand for both hardware and software in China and India. Successful leveraging of the interrelationships between different sectors, and between domestic firms and foreign multinationals, will be critical to the future success of the software industries in these three countries.

Acknowledgements

This case study is a reworked and enhanced version of material originally published in *Strategy Magazine* (McManus et al., 2007b) and *Asia-Pacific Business Review* (McManus, 2008).

Note

1. Comment made at a workshop on global software development, Reginald H. Jones Centre, Wharton School, December 1999.

8

Case study: evaluating the commercial aerospace industry of the BRIC nations

Introduction

The commercial aerospace industry has for many years been the province of Western manufacturers which have exported their products all across the globe. This dominance has arisen because of the high requirement for design, engineering and manufacturing expertise essential for these products. Many of the advanced techniques pioneered in the industry have now migrated to other industries as standard methods of production. Over the past 20 years a number of well-known manufacturers, such as Douglas and Lockheed, have disappeared from commercial aircraft production, and the market is now dominated by two major players: Boeing and Airbus between them control a significant proportion of the market for commercial aircraft. The battle for supremacy between these two companies has been well documented (Irwin and Pavcnik, 2004) and there have been many arguments about the degree of subsidy which each has enjoyed from their respective governments. Airbus is well known as a joint venture between a number of companies and, effectively, countries; what is possibly not so well known is that Boeing could not manufacture without extensive strategic alliances.

It is now unlikely that any single company will be able to produce commercial fleet aircraft successfully without these kinds of cooperative arrangements. Concentrating on the 110-seat-plus segment of the market, this case study addresses some of the issues that will be faced by the emerging countries in their efforts to establish a global presence in the commercial airline industry.

The global aerospace industry

The leading manufacturers estimate that the market for commercial aircraft between 2003 and 2020 will be worth $2 trillion at current prices. The industry is very concentrated, with the top two firms having 100 per cent global share of the 100-seat-plus commercial aircraft market (Morgan Stanley, 1998) and 74 per cent of the 20–90-seat market (Silvera, 2000), and the top three firms having virtually 100 per cent of the aero-engine market (Turpin, 1998). By 2005 the world's fleet of airliners exceeded 25,000 (Kingsley-Jones, 2005). The most popular aircraft was the Airbus A320 family with over 2,400 units, with the next two places being taken by Boeing 737 variants totalling 4,200 units. The next eight places were also taken by Boeing aircraft.

Typical prices for new aircraft are $100 million and $140 million for a Boeing 737 and Boeing 767 respectively (Jafri, 2004). The development cost of the Boeing 787 has been estimated at $6–8 billion, while the Airbus 380 is estimated to cost $12–18 billion (Barling, 2004). However, these costs are considered to be worth the risk since a successful airliner can lock up a market segment for at least 20 years. The Boeing 747 has enjoyed a monopoly in the 400-seat-plus category and generated $45 million profit for every aircraft sold (Nolan et al., 2007).

The global industry is known to be highly cyclical and tied to both the health and the profitability of the airline industry. There is, invariably, a time lag between traffic recovery and airline profitability, as excess capacity after delivery of new aircraft has to be absorbed by the airlines. For manufacturers there is an additional delay, since airlines only order new aircraft once they are confident of traffic forecasts; this is exacerbated by the build time of two years (Costa et al., 2002). Although airlines are currently profitable, the present recovery cycle in which the industry finds itself is forecast to peak in 2010 or 2011 (Fidler et al., 2004). Additionally, airlines 'mothball' aircraft when capacity persistently exceeds demand.

There are many drivers which affect the demand for civil aircraft: the main ones are aircraft retirements – typically an airframe can last 30 years; the number of passengers – forecast to increase steadily over the next decade but there are regional differences; and operators' revenue – currently the rising cost of fuel is being offset by efficiencies, and this may drive the need for newer, more efficient aircraft. Passenger growth has enabled airlines to outperform initial expectations for 2006 and cut their global losses, according to figures from the IATA, from just over $3 billion to about $500 million (Dunn, 2007a). Another factor is passenger taste – increasingly passengers wish to avoid the traditional hub-and-spoke approach and fly point to point directly to their destination.

Over the next 20 years Boeing (2004) predicts that there will be demand for 25,000 new aircraft, Airbus (2003) predicts 16,500 and Rolls-Royce, the engine manufacturer, predicts 41,000. The apparent contradiction in these figures arises because each manufacturer has different products suitable for different segments of the market. Additionally, there is uncertainty about the demand for business aircraft, a significant market for the Brazilian manufacturer Embraer, which may represent up to a third of the demand.

The industry is similar to the automobile industry in that manufacturers will produce aircraft by combining components such as fuselage, interior, engines and avionics from major suppliers, known as tier 1 firms, to produce the final product. As much as 32 per cent of the final product is sourced in this way (Stirton, 2003). There is an additional market for spares and repairs, and this tends to be served by tier 1 and 2 suppliers. Tier 1 firms are defined as system integrators, tier 2 as sub-system integrators, and beneath these are individual suppliers.

Airbus was originally a consortium of Aerospatiale (France), BAE Systems (UK), Deutsche Aerospace (Germany) and Construcciones Aeronauticas (Spain) but, after various reorganisations and political battles, is now controlled by a single company. The French, German and Spanish partners merged to create EADS. Airbus SAS became a fully integrated company with a single management structure in 2001 with two shareholders (EADS 80 per cent, BAE Systems 20 per cent). BAE Systems sold its stake in October 2006, since when Airbus has been wholly owned by EADS. Airbus has designed its aircraft in such a way that there is commonality across flight systems and, once trained to fly one aircraft, crew can pilot any Airbus plane. This is not the case with Boeing, where such 'fly-by-wire' technology is not incorporated in the aircraft.

Boeing operates a highly centralised manufacturing operation with strategic decisions taken in the USA. This is intended to produce global scale efficiencies. In order to ensure supply-chain efficiency, knowledge, in terms of technology and processes, flows from the centre to the regional subsidiaries. Boeing managers are based in each supplier organisation, with the remit of driving down manufacturing costs. This consistency of organisational design across all suppliers, regardless of where they are based, ensures that information flows from head office are disseminated quickly and flows of components back to the manufacturing plants are also rapid.

With the objective of sourcing fewer, but larger, sub-assemblies from suppliers, the company aims to focus on aircraft design and final assembly more effectively. The supply base has dropped from 1,900 firms in 2001 to 1,200 firms in 2006. This 40 per cent reduction means that many current lower-tier suppliers will have to build relationships with current tier 1 suppliers. At present Boeing works with 24 collaborative tier 1 partners based in ten different countries. Of the foreign countries only the UK (two), Japan (three) and China (eight) have multiple supplying firms. Not all these suppliers have been chosen for their technical expertise alone – the high number of Chinese suppliers is due to the size of the Chinese market and the strong negotiating position of the Chinese government. Invariably, because of the high cost of aircraft, purchase negotiations involve Boeing, the airline and the host government, which will be keen to see the price offset by future manufacturing opportunities for firms in its country. These industrial commitment dollars agreed during purchase negations lead to significant FDI by Boeing.

For the development of its next model, the 787, Boeing has taken the systems integrator model even further: over 90 per cent will be outsourced, including manufacturing and design processes, and distributed across an international risk-sharing partnership (MacPherson and Pritchard, 2003). While this offers financial advantages to Boeing, it has been argued that it is trading away intellectual property that has been accumulated over decades to risk-sharing partners (Pritchard and MacPherson, 2007). Since the cost of developing an aircraft is so high – the Boeing 777 cost $5 billion (Esposito, 2003) – this may be the only way forward for manufacturers bearing in mind the continuing discussions at the WTO between the EU and the US government (Dunn, 2007b).

By contrast to the approach used by Boeing, Airbus has traditionally operated a far looser consortium among its tier 1 suppliers, without embedded managers. However, for the next aircraft in development, the A350XWB, Airbus is also adopting the Boeing business model since this will allow it to invest less capital in the new launch programme compared to the self-funded launch programmes it has traditionally operated. The knowledge gained in research so far will be made public to the first- and second-tier suppliers. Since such risk-sharing partners will not be able to claim their additional development costs, they will spread them across the components they manufacture for other companies. Airbus argues that this process is necessary because, with 40–50 companies across its supply chain, it is becoming increasingly difficult to ensure final product quality.

Having identified knowledge management as a key enabler in reducing costs, improving quality and ensuring products produced at or above specification, Airbus has set up VIVACE (value improvement through a virtual aeronautical collaborative enterprise), a project focusing on simulation and modelling techniques for aeronautical products during the design and development phases, funded by an EU grant and involving the majority of Airbus suppliers. Knowledge will be shared across the extended enterprise. As an example of the unintended transfer of knowledge, the involvement of Spanish firm CASA in Airbus has allowed the firm to develop specific knowledge about the design of panel mountings, which it has used in a partnership with Dirganata of Indonesia. Dirganata is also a supplier to Boeing, for which it mounts panels (Esposito, 2003). Is this a stage in the process of industrial transformation described by Schumpeter (1942) as 'creative destruction'? Or will it lead to the strategic destruction of Western aircraft manufacturers and their transformation into companies that only market and sell aircraft?

In this volatile global marketplace, the BRIC nations have both strengths and weaknesses in developing their aeronautical industries (Table 8.1).

Table 8.1   PEST comparison of BRIC nations

	Brazil	Russia	India	China
Political climate	Increased regulatory reforms Increased political support and tax breaks Stronger political affiliations with Western governments Strong political support for domestic markets	Increased government financial and tax incentives for start-up firms Increased regulatory reforms Strong political motivation for globalisation	Adaptive legislative framework Strong tax incentives for inward investors Strong political motivation for globalisation Strong reputation and trust	Commitment to an adaptable tax regime Strong government focus for software industry Strong political support for domestic firms Strong financial incentives for start-up firms
Economic climate	Competitive labour-cost model Increasing growth rate in software sector Improved export position Improved infrastructure	Competitive labour-cost model Highly developed infrastructure Stronger macroeconomic policy Strong domestic market growth Strong potential for export growth	Adaptive and highly mobile workforce Adaptive investment regime Links to technological investments Competitive labour-cost model Strong export base Strong infrastructure	Adaptable labour force Adapting technical skills Quality of infrastructure Strong and expanding industrial sector Strong export focus

| Table 8.1 | PEST comparison of BRIC nations (*Cont'd*) | | | |

	Brazil	Russia	India	China
Societal climate	Increased employability in software markets Increased support for education Increased support for entrepreneurship	High-level specialist personnel Increased employability in software markets Improved English-speaking population	Adaptive English-speaking population Strong and highly developed educational culture Strong management culture	Commitment to training in scientific disciplines Strong social identity Strong education sector Strong local brand loyalty
Technological climate	Adaptive to new technologies and innovation Increasing number of science graduates (PhDs) Improving R&D culture Strong ties with Western technology companies	Adaptive technical workforce Increased ties with Western firms Strong R&D culture Strong linkages between universities and firms	Adaptive to new technologies Strong R&D culture Strong ties with Western technology companies Strong technical skills	Commitment to protecting intellectual property Increasing support for incubation units Long-term commitment to R&D Strong linkages between universities and firms

Source: McManus (2008)

Brazil's aerospace industry

Between 1992 and 2001 the Brazilian government completely deregulated the domestic airline industry, stimulating price competition and the entry of new companies into the industry. The first low-cost carrier, Gol, entered the market in 2003 to join the existing legacy carriers Varig, Vasp, TAM and Transbrasil. Gol's vice president for marketing, Tarcisio Gargioni, said: 'in 2000, out of the 170 million Brazilian population only 6 million flew commercial aviation. Out of the remainder, some 25 million could also become potential fliers provided prices were reduced 30 per cent' (Lima, 2002). By 2003 Brazil's domestic airline industry carried 30 million passengers, compared to 132 million passengers transported by interstate bus companies. The business travel segment of the market was the strongest and accounted for 70 per cent of the total domestic demand for air travel, with the ten busiest city routes accounting for over 35 per cent of traffic (Gol, 2005).

By early 2007 the airline market was undergoing extreme financial difficulties, and at the end of March Gol acquired Varig. The country has been left with two dominant airlines, Gol/Varig and TAM. This background does not present a strong demand forecast for locally manufactured aircraft.

Market capability

While Airbus and Boeing dominate the market for 100-plus-seat aircraft, Embraer and Bombardier of Canada control the market for regional jets, i.e. sub-100 seats. Of these two companies, Embraer is seen to be a far stronger competitor than Bombardier. Embraer was formed in 1969 and privatised by the Brazilian government in 1994. Although the company originally made 50–70-seat aircraft, since 1999 it has expanded into the 70–100-seat segments, which have been neglected by both Boeing and Airbus. Like Airbus, Embraer has focused on commonality of supplies and systems to enable airlines to minimise costs on inventories and crew training, and keep its own design and development costs to a minimum. Additionally it has employed the lean manufacturing concept adopted by Boeing, so it acts as a final-tier assembler for tier 1 and 2 suppliers. Embraer now competes at the bottom end of the larger market with the 98-seat ERJ-190 and 108-seat ERJ-195 and has, by securing an order from the US carrier JetBlue, broken the monopoly Airbus had with this airline (Fidler et al., 2004). Since these aircraft are designed specifically for these capacities, rather than the shrunken versions of larger aircraft offered by both Boeing and Airbus, they are significantly lighter and offer a more fuel-efficient aircraft.

Future potential

The majority of the beleaguered Brazilian airline industry purchases have been from Boeing. During the purchase negotiations the government has not been successful in securing industrial commitment dollars for the Brazilian aerospace industry. The prospects for the manufacture of, or contribution to the manufacture of, large commercial aircraft seem limited in the foreseeable future. However, for the smaller classes of aircraft the forecast is somewhat different. According to an Embraer analysis, from 2007 to 2016 the VLJ, light and mid-light categories will account for 45 per cent of all business jets (11,115 new aircraft worldwide worth $169 billion) delivered. Its total figures for Europe, Africa and the Middle East suggest that 2,125 (valued at $41 billion) new VLJ/L and ML aircraft will form 43 per cent of this market. The analysis does not even count a potential 2,500–3,000 air-taxi orders, or the market for regional jets which Embraer has entered both directly and through a number of joint ventures (Vines, 2007).

Russia's aerospace industry

Despite the trend of a downturn for the global aviation industry in 2000–2003, the Russian air transport market saw passenger numbers rise 14 per cent year on year in 2001, a further 6 per cent in 2002, 11 per cent in 2003 and nearly 16 per cent in 2004. Volume in 2005 reached 85.8 billion revenue passenger kilometres (RPKs) in Russia, while the number of passengers carried climbed to 35.1 million in total (Renaissance Securities, 2006). Russia's airline market showed sustained growth during the first half of 2007, with the top 20 carriers flying nearly 16 million passengers, 7.4 million of them on domestic flights (Zvereva, 2007). In the 1990s only two airlines operated foreign aircraft, but by the mid-2000s there were many more Boeing and Airbus aircraft in operation, replacing the less fuel-efficient and high MRO (maintenance, repair and overhaul) cost Russian aircraft. Many of the older aircraft do not comply with modern air-safety requirements. Despite the current high trade barriers imposed to protect the domestic aerospace industry, by 2015 Aeroflot, the largest Russian carrier, expects to have 44–45 long-haul aircraft, mainly Boeing 787s and Airbus A350s. By the same time the company expects to have 56 Airbus A32s and 45 Sukhoi Superjets in operation on regional flights. Sukhoi was not the only domestic manufacturer to make sales to Russian airlines, with both Antonov (31 aircraft) and Tupolev (21 aircraft) announcing sales to be delivered over the next decade to other carriers. Additionally a tender agreement between Antonov, Sukhoi, Bombardier and Embraer was announced for 30 regional aircraft for delivery by 2012. In all cases state-appointed representatives on the board of directors would have a prominent opinion on which supplier should be selected. Airbus already has a number of agreements in place with Russia's United Aircraft Corporation for the development and manufacture of components locally.

Market capability

Russia's civil aviation industry has gone through the most difficult period in its history. Originally established to supply the Soviet military, Russia's aerospace industry employed some 1.5 million people in 1990, accounting for more than 25 per cent of the world's civil and 40 per cent of the military production of aircraft. The civil aviation sector dropped dramatically in the 1990s, falling from production of 500 airplanes and 215 helicopters in 1990 to only 14 and 40 respectively in 1998. In 1999 Russia manufactured nine civilian aircraft and 21 military planes, but production of civilian aircraft dropped to four in 2000.

The Russian aircraft industry was by then highly fragmented, consisting of approximately 300 design bureaus, plants and research facilities. These included ten major aircraft designers and over 20 major manufacturing facilities involved in military and civil production. There was a rich heritage of design and construction of both commercial aviation and space products, and a continuing capability to produce a wide range of airplanes and rockets. But in addition to common economic difficulties, the Russian aircraft industry faces a number of specific problems.

Historically, the domestic civil aircraft industry was generally unresponsive to the needs of the marketplace. Development of new aircraft took place in an isolated environment, and was driven largely by a desire to hone the technical capabilities and ambitions of design bureaus. These tended to build aircraft similar to Western analogues, not directly in response to the market potential of the aircraft. Thus the domestic industry, having an excessive number of aircraft design facilities, created a wide variety of aircraft types – exceeding the number of types developed by the rest of the world. With consolidation within the industry and the formation of United Aircraft Corporation in 2006, together with a clearer policy from the government, it may be that former levels of productivity can be achieved. This consolidation encompassed the top level of the industry, and by August 2007 there were attempts to consolidate the first-tier suppliers – particularly engine manufacturers (Lantratov and Gritskova, 2007). The state no longer directly controls the industry, due to the sale of shares in the leading aircraft manufacturers starting from 1992, but most boards of directors have state-appointed members.

Future potential

Russian airline involvement in the privatisation of European airlines will present opportunities for Russian manufacturers in the longer term. Aeroflot's bid for Alitalia and its offer to buy Serbia's JAT Airways, along with AirUnion's winning tender for the privatised Hungarian national airline Malev, would make Russia a significant presence within both Europe and the SkyTeam airline consortium.

Russia's ability to manufacture is currently developing, but is heavily dependent upon joint ventures with foreign companies for its success. A joint venture between Irkut (formerly Yakolev), Tupolev and Ilyushin will develop the MS-21 aircraft: a medium/short-haul carrier offering 150-, 170-, 180- and 210-seat planes. Authorisation of preliminary design is scheduled for 2009 and technical design should be finished by 2010, with the first deliveries by 2015. With the intention to make most of the aircraft from composites, manufacturing technology will have to be purchased, and it is likely that the engines will be either an outright purchase from Rolls-Royce or manufactured in Russia by a joint venture between Perm (a Russian firm) and Pratt & Witney. There are currently doubts about Perm's ability to make a contribution to the project.

The area where Russia does enjoy an advantage, and a greater potential advantage, is through its world leadership in the production of titanium. Titanium parts make up approximately 15 per cent of the Boeing 787 airframe and mainly come from Russia. Boeing and VSMPO-AVISMA announced in April 2006 a joint venture to start primary machining of titanium castings prior to their shipment to the USA for finishing; presently VSMPO-AVISMA only supplies untreated castings. First shipments are expected to be delivered from a $60 million purpose-built facility in 2008. It seems that Russia's progress will be very dependent upon joint ventures and the import of technology if it is to compete on the aerospace world stage.

India's aerospace industry

Over 100 airlines operated in the Indian airline industry immediately after the Second World War (Brimson, 1985). The intense competition was destructive, and the Indian government nationalised the industry in the 1950s. Controls started to be relaxed in 1986 and have continued to relax, such that by 1996 private airlines carried more than 40 per cent of total passengers. However, there was still an uncertain climate in the industry, and in 1997 both Kuwait Airlines and Gulf Air were required to divest their interests in Jet Airways, the largest private Indian airline.

In 2007 the government allowed consolidation within the industry to combat increasing competition and sustained losses being made by nearly all airlines. Collectively, the airlines announced losses of $500 million during 2007 and are not expected to post a profit until 2010 (Jariwala, 2007). The consolidation has led to three major groups: Air India, Air India Express and Indian Airlines, which is state run; Jet Airways (India) and JetLite; and lastly Kingfisher Airlines, which has a 46 per cent stake in Air Deccan (the low-cost airline) run by United Breweries Group (Luthra, 2007).

Together the three groups control approximately 85 per cent of the domestic market, which represented 32 million passengers in 2006. The government also announced that the requirement for airlines to operate domestic flights for five years before undertaking international flights would be abandoned. The civil aviation minister, Praful Patel, said 'We want to take Indian carriers' inbound and outbound market share to 50 per cent, which can only be achieved by encouraging our airlines to fly abroad' (Kumar, 2007). The minister forecast that there would be significant growth in the domestic market, which should reach 182 million passengers by 2020. Airbus and Boeing increased their earlier forecasts, saying respectively that India's airlines would need 1,100 and 856 aircraft between 2006 and 2025.

Market capability

The Indian aerospace industry is dominated by the state-run Hindustan Aeronautics (HAL), where the main emphasis has been on the defence industry. Before its collapse the Soviet Union was the primary partner. HAL has a long history of collaboration with several other international and domestic aerospace agencies, such as the Sukhoi Aviation Corporation, Israel Aircraft Industries, Mikoyan-Gurevich, BAE Systems, Dassault Aviation, Dornier Flugzeugwerke, Aeronautical Development Agency Aerospatielle and the Indian Space Research Organisation. These relationships have been as either a licensed manufacturer or a subcontractor – particularly in the case of Boeing and Airbus. In essence India is still a country that is predominantly dependent on foreign imports of aircraft and aircraft parts.

Commercial aircraft builders like Boeing and Airbus and defence aeronautic companies such as Dassault and Lockheed have significant market control of the Indian A&D

(aerospace and defence) space. However, the government is spending considerable resources to enable the growth of local capacity to capitalise on what it believes to be a lucrative industry, especially as it tries to establish self-reliance and improve exports. Despite this, more than 80 per cent of commercial aircraft and parts are imported, highlighting the continued dependence on foreign suppliers. The USA accounted for about 35 per cent of imports in 2004–2005.

HAL is currently working as a subcontractor to Airbus for the A320 (door panels) and hopes to be involved in the A380 and the ATR 42/72 (a joint venture between EADS and Italy's Alenia) (Jasper, 2001). Part of its contribution comes via its software development ability being applied to wing design products. At the end of 2007 Airbus announced the opening of a training and engineering centre in Bangalore, and a memorandum of understanding was signed with Boeing to seek out $1 billion of manufacturing cooperation over the following decade. Part of this opportunity may be the conversion of Boeing 737s to cargo planes as they become too old to carry passengers. There are estimated to be 3,000 such conversions in the pipeline between now and 2025. Additionally, an agreement between VSMPO-AVISMA Corporation and Kerala Minerals was made to build a titanium smelter with a capacity of 10,000 tonnes per annum to supply HAL.

Future potential

The Indian economy is one the fastest growing in the world, reflecting the successful reform process initiated in 1991, and the government has gradually opened key sectors to foreign participation and investment.

There are five key levers driving growth in India's A&D industry: a rapidly growing commercial aviation sector, particularly with the arrival of low-cost carriers such as

Air Deccan; a significantly large aerospace defence budget; foreign players increasingly outsourcing parts' manufacturing, IT and engineering services; the government's increased role in promoting the industry; and finally a domestic set of private players that are attempting to reshape aircraft manufacturing and design. There are also challenges that could potentially hinder progress in the A&D industry. The Indian government's lack of both transparency and speed in decision-making makes transactions difficult for aircraft manufacturers supplying this powerful body. Additionally, an immature MRO infrastructure could limit growth of carriers in terms of flight frequency and additional routes, thereby adversely affecting demand for aircraft and parts.

With increasing outsourcing opportunities, the Indian aerospace industry could emerge as a key participant in the Asia-Pacific market. Apart from India's perceived viability as an outsourcing hub for aerospace and defence products, the overwhelming involvement of the government in areas of supply and demand cements its advantage in the industry. The government's proactive soliciting of international cooperation may see production moving to India, generating more opportunities for the country. In the first half of 2006 Indian corporations spent over £1.1 billion on 29 international acquisitions (Neveling, 2006). This followed a similarly acquisitive 2005, when £2 billion was paid for 42 foreign companies. This may mean that technology and manufacturing capabilities in the aerospace industry are acquired by purchase as well as by transfer through partnership.

China's aerospace industry

Currently the potential for regional jets in the Chinese market is high. The airline industry has expanded at 18 per cent per annum since 1978, and more than 90 feeder airlines have been developed to serve the mainland's medium-sized cities in recent years, operating 570 general aviation aircraft (Xiao, 2006). In most major airline markets approximately 30 per cent of aircraft are regional jets with fewer than 100 seats; the figure in China is currently 12 per cent. It has been estimated that by 2020 regional aircraft will comprise 600 of a total of over 1,800 aircraft. Current statistics suggest that 60 per cent of flights range between 600 and 2,200 kilometres and on average 8 per cent carry fewer than 100 passengers. Chinese national and international carriers currently use large aircraft capable of carrying more than 150 passengers, purchasing their airplanes from Boeing and Airbus. The government was quoted as saying:

> Transport by regional jets will become the new growth area of the country's civil aviation industry. China would give top priority to the research and development of regional aircraft in the coming decades. Production of regional airliners is the best choice for the nation as the aviation industry currently lacks the capability of producing larger passenger aircraft competitively. (*People's Daily Online*, 2004)

Market capability

The market for regional jets is principally served by two companies: Embraer of Brazil and Bombardier of Canada – of these, Bombardier is believed to be the weaker. China has approached this market in two ways. Firstly, the China Aviation Industry Corporation I (AVIC I)[1] has launched the ARJ-21 series with two versions: one capable of carrying 75 passengers, and the other 85. To date orders have been placed by domestic carriers for 71 aircraft (*People's Daily Online*, 2007a) and the first deliveries are scheduled for September 2008. AVIC I intends to export 150 ARJ-21 aircraft by 2020. Although the aircraft has been designed in China, initially engines and many other components will be manufactured abroad. Secondly, AVIC II, a different consortium, has signed an agreement with Embraer to produce the ERJ154, a 30–50-seat aircraft, and the joint venture has already successfully supplied aircraft to some of the country's regional airlines.

Regarding larger aircraft, although China is not yet capable of building these, it has supplied sub-components to Boeing since 1980, and more recently to Airbus. The quality of engineering and workmanship has risen dramatically and there are approximately 3,300 Boeing aircraft flying which include major parts built in China. Technological competitiveness has been added to low-cost manufacturing skills. There are now 19 separate supply organisations working with Boeing from 13 locations in China.

Future potential

The future potential for Chinese aircraft manufacturing is high. The government negotiates forcefully when aircraft are purchased for domestic airlines, as mentioned earlier. Additionally, AVIC I is a strong organisation which now comprises 53 large and medium-sized manufacturers, 30 research institutes and 30 specialised institutes and organisations which, between them, supply components to all the major aircraft manufacturers in the world. In Shaanxi province, where most production takes place, there are more than 30 universities with 900,000 students, and almost 300,000 aircraft workers. Most notably, AVIC I is the anchor firm in the new Xi'an high-tech park, a 40 square kilometre special high-tech aviation zone currently under construction. The park is designed to attract aviation parts and component manufacturers from all over the world through joint ventures, and provide the tipping point for China's aviation industry. Similarly, AVIC II comprises 54 large to medium-sized organisations, a further 22 organisations and three research institutes, and employs over 210,000 workers.

The country already has the main drivers for large aircraft manufacture. For example:

- it is becoming one of the largest, if not the largest, domestic and international passenger markets of the world;

- it already has the largest demand for regional and medium-sized aircraft in the world;

- China's military aircraft infrastructure gives its commercial industry a technology, design and scale advantage second only to the USA and Europe;

- aviation is one of the fixed-investment, high-margin industries that could drive China's export potential over the coming decades;

- the cluster being built in the Xi'an park has the potential to support the efficient expansion of the industry;

- the country has an unparalleled pool of talented engineers and aerospace scientists, superior to any other country;

- China's high-tech, low-cost development and manufacturing can break the duopoly of Boeing and Airbus.

As we move towards the end of the first decade of the twenty-first century, China has started to make acquisitions of companies that it needs to progress its economic development – it cannot be much longer before those acquisitions include foreign aerospace companies.

Conclusion

Any strong development of the aerospace industry within the BRIC nations will be dependent upon foreign companies, notably Boeing and Airbus. There are a number of factors which affect the growth of the aerospace industry within the BRIC nations: the most important of these would seem to be demand and the respective political situations. There is no doubt that the skill base within India and Brazil is as strong as that within both China and Russia. However, the governments of both China and Russia are prepared to negotiate aggressively with foreign companies to ensure that FDI brings with it technology transfer. Both countries also have strong demand and growth prospects for their airline industries. While India has similar growth potential, it has not made FDI so easy for foreign companies, and the airline industry within Brazil is currently stagnating. Embraer of Brazil enjoys sales on a global scale, but only in a small section of the market. How long it will take the other countries to follow is uncertain, but it is certain that they will.

Note

1. AVIC I is a consortium formed by Chengdu Aircraft Industry Group, Shanghai Aircraft Company, Shenyang Aircraft Corporation and Xian Aircraft Company.

9

Conclusion

This book has attempted to present a timely new perspective on the challenges faced by global organisations and their managers undertaking business within a complex and changing world economy. Without doubt the twentieth-century business model based on Adam Smith's (1776) representation of consumption and self-interest is not working – maximising utility within the framework of the market economy is divisive and propagates inequality. It could be argued that the next decade will be typified by those organisations that embrace a model of openness, conservation, moral entrepreneurship and ethical and social responsibility.

It is sometimes forgotten that Adam Smith (1759) published a 'theory of moral sentiments' examining altruistic sentiments – and adjusting to the challenges of twenty-first-century globalisation will require firms to embrace altruism on an unprecedented scale. If we accept that globalisation is integration at the world level, firms will have to operate in an increasingly cooperative manner, as technology increases the mobility of individuals and deregulation becomes more widespread.

Another challenge for twenty-first-century nation-states, and firms operating within these nation-states, is the absorption and spreading of knowledge capital. Over the next years and decades the absorption of new technology, especially mobile technologies and multimedia, will play an increasing role in liberalising restricted business practices. In theory at least, this will create investment opportunities for those countries with surplus (hard) currency, such as China and India.

The notion of liberalising markets and free-market democracies will present enormous challenges for the G8 economies. Fitting China into the world economy is not without its risks – although China has a huge banking sector, private firms in China are among the most dependent in the world on internally generated capital. China's partial reforms, while successful in increasing the scope of the market, have so far failed to address much inefficiency in the Chinese economy.

For the years ahead, the areas of economic growth will be Brazil, Russia, India and China (the BRIC nations). Their growing economic stature means the BRIC nations are emerging as competitors to the USA, Europe and Japan. Arguably, it is in the economic interests of the USA to concentrate on forming economic alliances with Brazil and China. Some economic thinkers argue that the USA should forgo its current European partnerships in favour of a new America-Japan-China alliance.

The potential decline of the nation-state, together with the increasing interaction and integration of national economic systems through growth in international trade, markets, investment and capital flows, presents opportunities and possibilities for governments, institutions, firms, individuals and entrepreneurs – far greater than have been seen in the last 100 years.

In conclusion, we hope that you have found this book interesting and insightful, and have enjoyed reading it as much as we have enjoyed researching and writing it.

References

Abdullah, A. and Singh, S. (1992) 'Leading and motivating', in A. Abdullah (ed.) *Understanding the Malaysian Workforce. Guidelines for Managers.* Kuala Lumpur: Malaysian Institute of Management, pp. 33–48.

Airbus (2003) *Global Market Forecast 2003–2022.* Cedex: Airbus S.S.S.

Allan, J., Fairtlough, G. and Heinzen, B. (2002) *The Power of the Tale: Using Narratives for Organisational Success.* Chichester: John Wiley & Sons.

Ansoff, Igor (1990) *Implementing Strategic Management.* New York: Prentice-Hall.

Ballon, P. (2006) 'Business modelling for ICT products and services: conceptual framework and design criteria', in S. Limonard, P. Ballon, R. Tee and U. Wehn de Montalvo (eds) *Integrated Methodological Framework: Investigating Business Models for Broadband Services in the Case of iDTV Platforms.* Enschede: Freeband; available at: *www.freeband.nl/* (accessed: 19 May 2008).

Barling, Russell (2004) 'Aircraft giants in war of words: Airbus and Boeing hit a spot of turbulence over each other's marketing tactics', *South China Morning Post,* 29 March; available at: *http://archive.scmp.com/results.php* (accessed: 12 May 2008).

Bartlett, C.A. and Ghoshal, S. (1989) *Managing Across Borders.* Boston, MA: Harvard Business School Press.

Berhin, D. (2005) 'Knowledge sharing and learning organisations: the McKinsey & Co experience', paper presented at Strategic Knowledge Management Forum, London, November, unpublished.

Bertrand, Gilles, Michalski, Anna and Pench, Lucio R. (1999) 'Scenarios Europe 2010: five possible futures for Europe', working paper, July. Brussels: European Commission Forward Studies Unit.

Blomstermo, A. and Deo Sharma, D. (2005) 'Choice of foreign entry mode in service firms', *International Marketing Review*, 23(2): 211–29.

Blundell, John (2006) 'Core values', *The Business*, 4 June.

Boeing (2004) 'Current market outlook: executive overview', Boeing Commercial Airplanes; available at: *www.boeing.com/commercial/cmo/1-2.html* (accessed: 12 November 2007).

Botten, N. and McManus, J. (1999) *Competitive Strategies for Services Organisations*. Basingstoke: Macmillan.

Bridgewater, S. (2000) 'Strategic management in emerging markets', in M. Tayeb (ed.) *International Business*. London: Financial Times/Prentice-Hall, pp. 340–53.

Brimson, S. (1985) *The Airlines of the World*. Sydney: Dreamweaver Books.

Brown, James (2006) 'Information technology', *Computing*, 9 November, p. 23.

Business Week (2006) 'Oil prices: the new reality. Futures traders are already assuming sky-high prices are here to stay', *Business Week*, 6 February.

Canals, J. (1999) 'Scale versus specialisation: banking strategies after the euro', *European Management Journal*, 17(6): 566–75.

Carlsson, B., Jacobsson, S., Holmén, M. and Rickne, A. (2002) 'Innovation systems: analytical and methodological issues', *Research Policy*, 31: 233–45.

Chandler, Alfred (1965) *Railroads, The Nation's First Big Business*. New York: Columbia University Press.

Chesbrough, Henry (2006) *Open Business Models*. Boston, MA: Harvard Business School Press.

Chung, T.Z. (1991) 'Culture: a key to management between the Asia-Pacific area and Europe', *European Management Journal*, 9(4): 419–24.

Clark, T.H. and Lee, H.G. (1998) 'Security First Network Bank: a case study of an internet pioneer', *Proceedings of 31st Hawaii International Conference on System Sciences*, Vol. 4. Honolulu: University of Hawaii College of Business Administration, pp. 73–82.

Clarke, G. (2001) 'Good to great, interview with Jim Collins', *Fast Company.com*, 51, September; available at: *www.fastcompany.com/magazine/51/goodtogreat.html* (accessed: 5 May 2008).

Cohen, Eliot A. and Gooch, John (1990) *Military Misfortunes: The Anatomy of Failure in War*. New York: Free Press, pp. 59–133.

Collins, J. (2001) *Good to be Great*. New York: Harper Business.

Computing Business (2007) 'Stand out from the crowd', *Computing Business*, February; available at: *www.computingbusiness.co.uk/archives* (accessed: 12 May 2008).

Costa, P., Harned, D. and Lindquist, J. (2002) 'Rethinking the aviation industry', *McKinsey Quarterly*, Special Edition, Risk and Resilience; available at: *www.mckinseyquarterly.com/Rethinking_the_aviation_industry_1190* (accessed: 5 May 2008).

Cummins, Chip, Warren, Susan, Burrionuevo, Alexei and Bahee, Bhushan (2004) 'Losing reserve: at Shell, strategy and structure fueled troubles', *Wall Street Journal*, 12 March, p. A1.

Daft, D. (2000) 'Back to classic Coke', *Financial Times*, 27 March, p. 20.

Deutsch, C.M. (1997) 'Fuji builds a brand as rival fumes about price', *New York Times*, 11 December, p. D1.

Dicken, Peter (1998) *Global Shift*. London: Paul Chapman.

Djankov, S. and McLiesh, C. (2005) *Doing Business in 2005: Removing Obstacles to Growth*. Oxford: World Bank/International Finance Corporation/Oxford University Press.

DM Review (2005) 'Unisys announces strategy aimed at driving profitable growth', *DM Review*, 4 November; available at: *www.dmreview.com/news/1041213-1.html* (accessed: 5 May 2008).

Drucker, P.F. (1954) *The Practice of Management*. New York: Harper & Row.

Drucker, P.F. (1992) *Managing for the Future*. New York: Butterworth-Heinemann.

Duarte, C. (2002) 'Brazil: cooperative development of a software industry', *IEEE Software*, May/June: 84–7.

Duarte, C. and Branco, C. (2001) 'Social and economic impacts of the Brazilian policy for information technologies', *Revista do BNDES*, 8(15): 125–45.

Duncan, Gary (2005) 'Economic review', *The Times*, 19 December; available at: *http://timesnews.typepad.com/news/2005/12/index.html* (accessed: 5 May 2008).

Dunn, Graham (2007a) 'Forecasts for 2007', *Flight International*, February.

Dunn, Graham (2007b) 'EC puts forward counter case in WTO Airbus-Boeing dispute', *Flight Global*, 27 September; available at: *www.flightglobal.com/articles/ 2007/09/27/ 217255/ec-puts-forward-counter-case-in-wto-airbus-boeing-dispute.html* (accessed: 27 December 2007).

Dutta, S. and Segev, A. (1999) 'Business transformation on the internet', *European Management Journal*, 17: 466–76.

Esposito, E. (2003) 'Strategic alliances and internationalisation in the aircraft manufacturing industry', *Technological Forecasting and Social Change*, 71: 443–68.

Ferris, T. (1988) *Coming of Age in the Milky Way*. New York: William Morrow.

Fidler, B., Mercay, C. and Laver, F. (2004) 'Global aerospace and defence review and industry focus', *DeutschBank Global Equity Research*, 19 January.

Foster, David (1998) *Managing Across Cultures*. Lincoln: University of Lincolnshire and Humberside.

Garr, Doug (2000) *IBM Redux: Lou Gerstner and the Business Turnaround of the Decade*. Hoboken, NJ: John Wiley & Sons.

General Electric (2006) *Annual Report 2006*. Fairfield, CT: General Electric Company; available at: *www.ge.com* (accessed: 5 May 2008).

Gol (2005) 'Prospectus for floatation of Gol preference shares', 27 April. Oslo: Pareto Securities.

Goldman Sachs (2003) 'Dreaming with BRICs: the path to 2050', Global Economics Paper No. 99. New York: Goldman Sachs, October.

Goldsmith, M., Greenberg, C.L., Robertson, A. and Hu-Chan, M. (2003) *Global Leadership: The Next Generation*. Upper Saddle River, NJ: Prentice-Hall.

Gopinath, G.R. (2004) 'Air Deccan topic: the revolution of low-fare air travel', paper presented at National Institute of Advanced Studies, Indian Institute of Science, Bangalore, 23 January.

Govindarajan, V. and Gupta, A. (2000) 'Analysis of the emerging global arena', *European Management Journal*, 8(3): 274–84.

Graham, E.M. and Wada, E. (2001) *Foreign Direct Investment in China: Effects on Growth and Economic Performance*. Canberra: Australia National University.

Gray, David (ed.) (2006) *Business Studies Update: 2006*. Lincoln: Lincoln University.

Gupta, J.K. (2006) 'Investment in aircraft production would add impetus to the economy', *Financial Express*, August; available at: *www.financialexpress.com/* (accessed: 28 November 2007).

Harris, Jerry (2001) 'Information technology and global class formation', September; available at: *http://net4dem .org/mayglobal/Papers/JerryHarris_UKPaper.pdf* (accessed: 5 May 2008).

Harvey Jones, John (2005) 'The third IDEAS talk', Newmarket, 18 July; available at: *www.spaceforideas .uk.com* (accessed: 5 May 2008).

Hatzichronoglou, T. (1996) 'Globalisation and competitiveness: relevant indicators', STI Working Paper. Paris: OECD Directorate for Science, Technology and Industry.

Hill, Charles (2001) *International Business Competing in the Global Marketplace*. Maidenhead: McGraw-Hill.

Hofstede, Geert (1980) *Culture's Consequences: International Differences in Work Related Values*. London: Sage Publications.

Hofstede, Geert (1991) *Cultures and Organizations: Software for the Mind*. New York: McGraw-Hill.

Holstein, William J. (2005) 'Are business schools failing the world?', *New York Times*, 19 June.

Huijser, Mijnd (2006) *The Cultural Advantage: A New Model for Succeeding with Global Teams*. Boston, MA: Intercultural Press.

Huo, Y.P. and Steers, R.M. (1993) 'Cultural influences on the design of incentive systems: the case of Asia', *Pacific Journal of Management*, 10(1): 71–85.

Hurni, M.L. (1955) 'Decision making in the age of automation', *Harvard Business Review*, 33(5): 49–58.

IBM (2006) *Expanding the Innovation Horizon: Global CEO Study*. St Leonards, NSW: IBM Australia.

Irwin, D.A. and Pavcnik, N. (2004) 'Airbus versus Boeing revisited: international competition in the aircraft market', *Journal of International Economics*, 64: 223–45.

Jafri, H. (2004) 'B7E7 list prices starts from low base', *Aircraft Value News*, 12(5); available at: *www.aviationtoday.com/avn/categories/commercial/3439.html* (accessed: 5 May 2008).

Jansen, Wendy, Steenbakkers, Wilchard and Jägers, Hans (2007) *New Business Models for the Knowledge Economy*. Aldershot: Gower Publishing.

Jariwala, M. (2007) 'Indian aviation consolidation spree', *International Aerospace*, May/June: 20–3.

Jasper, C. (2001) 'Indian aerospace: partners wanted', *Flight International*, 23 January; available at: *http://info.flightinternational.com* (accessed: 5 May 2008).

Johansson, J.K. (1997) *Global Marketing, Foreign Entry, Local Marketing and Global Management*. Chicago, IL: McGraw-Hill.

Kelly, Neon (2007) 'Interview with Peter Norvig, director of research for Google', *Computing*, November, p. 30.

Kidd, J.B. (2001) 'Discovering inter-cultural perceptual differences in MNEs', *Journal of Managerial Psychology*, 16(2): 106–26.

Kingsley-Jones, M. (2005) 'Counting tails', *Flight International*, 5 September; available at: *http://info.flightinternational.com* (accessed: 5 May 2008).

Koch, A.J. (2001) 'Selecting overseas markets and entry modes: two decision processes or one?', *Market Intelligence & Planning*, 19(1): 65–75.

Kokko, A., Tansini, R. and Zejan, M. (2001) 'Trade regimes and spillover effects of FDI: evidence from Uruguay', *Weltwirtschaftliches Archiv/Review of World Economics*, 137: 1–49.

Kotler, P., Asplund, C., Rein, I. and Haider, D. (1999) *Marketing Places: Europe. Attracting Investments, Industries, Residents and Visitors to European Cities, Communities, Regions and Nations.* Harlow: Prentice-Hall.

KPMG (2005) *International Annual Review 2005.* London: KPMG.

Kumar, N. (2007) 'Airlines may get to fly abroad before 5 years', *Economic Times (India)*, 27 August; available at: *http://timesofindia.indiatimes.com/* (accessed: 5 May 2008).

Lantratov, Konstantin and Gritskova, Alexandra (2007) 'Iran shields its nuclear activities by Russian missiles', *Kommersant Russia's Daily Online*, 27 December; available at: *http://212.248.33.60/* (accessed: 5 May 2008).

Le Roux, Pieter (1997) 'The Mont Fleur scenarios', *Deeper News*, 7(1).

Lennard, David M. (2006) 'Through the wall: a cross-cultural guide to doing business in China', *Asia Times*, June; available at: *www.atimes.com/atimes/Others/china-culture-guide.html* (accessed: 5 May 2008).

Levitt, Theodore (1983) 'The globalization of markets', *Harvard Business Review*, May–June: 92–102.

Lima, E. (2002) 'Brazil's daring wings', *Air Transport World*, May: 1–5.

Liss, Kenneth (2000) 'Entrepreneurship in Europe', presentation at Harvard Business School, Boston, MA, July.

Lu, Q. (2001) 'Learning and innovation in a transitional economy', *International Journal of Entrepreneurship and Innovation Management*, 1: 125–41.

Luthra, N. (2007) 'Consolidation to boost India airlines; tough challenges', *Dow Jones International News*, 5 November.

MacPherson, A. and Pritchard, D. (2003) 'The international decentralisation of US commercial aircraft production: implications for US employment and trade', *Futures*, 35: 221–38.

Maerki, Hans Ulrich (2007) 'The European patent forum: the IP landscape in 2025', paper presented to European Foundation for Management Development meeting, Barcelona, 18–19 April, unpublished.

Malkin, L. (1994) 'Ford reorganizes globally for era of the "world car"', *International Herald Tribune*, 22 April; available at: *www.iht.com/articles/1994/04/22/ford_0 .php* (accessed: 5 May 2008).

Mang, Paul (2000) 'Strategic innovation: Constantinos Markides on strategy and management', *Academy of Management Executives*, 14(3): 43.

Mannheim Innovation Panel (1999) *Services in the Future – Innovation Activities in the Services Sector*. Mannheim: Centre for European Economic Research.

McGrath, M. and More, E. (2002) *Forging and Managing Online Collaboration: The ITOL Experience*. Canberra: National Office for the Information Economy.

McManus, J. (1997) *Re-engineering Your Business*. London: Pitman Publishing.

McManus, J. (2008) 'The global software industry: evaluating the software markets of the BRIC nations', *Asia-Pacific Business Review*, 3(2): 1–9.

McManus, J. and Botten, N. (2006) 'Competitive analysis: thinking beyond stage one', *Management Services Journal*, Summer: 10–15.

McManus, J., Li, M. and Moitra, D. (2007a) *China and India: Opportunities and Threats for the Global Software Industry*. Oxford: Chandos Publishing.

McManus, J., Li, M. and Moitra, D. (2007b) 'Software industry in China and India', *Strategy Magazine*, 13: 25–8.

Mead, M. (1970) *Culture and Commitment*. New York: Natural History Press, Doubleday & Co.

METI (2001) *White Paper on Small, Medium Sized Enterprises in Japan*. Tokyo: Japanese Small Business Research Institute.

Mintzberg, Henry (1994) *The Rise and Fall of Strategic Planning*. Hemel Hempstead: Prentice-Hall International.

Morgan Stanley (1998) *The Competitive Edge*. New York and London: MSDW.

Neave, Henry R. (2000) 'The Deming dimension: management for a better future', inaugural professorial lecture, W. Edwards Deming Professor of Management, Nottingham Business School, Nottingham Trent University, 2 March.

Nesbitt, John (1994) *The Global Paradox*. New York: William Morrow.

Neveling, N. (2006) 'Indian companies go shopping', *Accountancy Age*, 25 May, p. 11.

Neville, Margaret (2004) 'Spiritual coaching, my online journal'; available at: *www.margaretneville.com/blog/2004_09_01_* (accessed: 8 May 2008).

Nolan, P., Zhang, J. and Liu, C. (2007) *The Global Business Revolution and the Cascade Effect*. Basingstoke: Palgrave Macmillan.

O Globo (2007) 'Múltis brasileiras crescem mais no exterior', *O Globo*, 21 January.

Obstfeld, Maurice and Taylor, Alan M. (2004) *Global Capital Markets: Integration, Crisis and Growth*. New York: Cambridge University Press.

OECD (1997) *The OECD Report on Regulatory Reform*. Paris: OECD.

OECD (2006) *Science and Engineering Indicators 2006*. Arlington, VA: National Science Foundation.

Office for South East Europe (2004) 'Speech by Mr Shengman Zhang, World Bank Managing Director, at the Mostar Old Bridge Ceremony, Mostar', 23 July. Brussels: European Commission/World Bank Office for South East Europe.

Ohmae, Kenichi (1982) *The Mind of the Strategist*. New York: McGraw-Hill.

Ohmae, Kenichi (1990) *The Borderless World*. New York: Harper Business.

Oman, C. (1996) 'The policy challenges of globalisation and regionalisation', Policy Brief No. 11. Paris: OECD Development Centre.

Oswald, Laura (1996) 'The place and space of consumption in a material world', *Design Issues*, 12(1): 48–62.

Palmer, A. and Cole, C. (1995) *Principles of Service Marketing*. Englewood Cliffs, NJ: McGraw-Hill.

Palmisano, Samuel (2006) 'The globally integrated enterprise', *Foreign Affairs*, June: 127.

Pappe, Y. and Drankina, E. (2007) 'How Russia is nationalised: the oil sector', *Alexander's Gas & Oil Connections*, 12 October; available at: *www.gasandoil .com/goc/frame_ntr_news.htm* (accessed: 5 May 2008).

Pavlotsky, D. (2007) 'Rapid Russian GDP growth opens new opportunities', 12 November; available at: *www.reksoft.com* (accessed: 8 January 2008).

People's Daily Online (2004) 'Economy vehicles showing growth for AviChina', *People's Daily Online*, 25 June; available at: *www.english.people.com.cn* (accessed: 5 May 2008).

People's Daily Online (2007a) 'China needs 630 more regional jets in next two decades', *People's Daily Online*, 2 September; available at: *www.english.people.com.cn* (accessed: 5 May 2008).

People's Daily Online (2007b) 'Race is on to get plane project off the ground, *People's Daily Online*, 13 July; available at: *http://english.people.com.cn/90001/90776/90884/6344298.html* (accessed: 24 January 2008).

Peters, Tom and Waterman, Robert (1982) *In Search of Excellence – Lessons from America's Best Run Companies*. Sydney: Harper & Row.

Porter, Michael E. (1980) *Competitive Strategy*. New York: Free Press.

Porter, Michael E. (ed.) (1986) *Competition in Global Industries*. Boston, MA: Harvard Business School Press.

Porter, Michael E. (1990) *The Competitive Advantage of Nations*. New York: Free Press.

Porter, Michael E. (1998) *Competitive Strategy: Techniques for Analyzing Industries and Competitors*. New York: Free Press.

Postman, N. (1993) *Technology – The Surrender of Culture to Technology*. New York: Vintage Books.

Pratt, Joanne H. (2002) *E-Biz: Strategies for Small Business Success*. Dallas, TX: SBA Office of Advocacy.

PriceWaterhouseCoopers (2005) 'Escalating deals', PriceWaterhouseCoopers; available at: *www.pwc.com/mandace* (accessed: 5 May 2008).

Pritchard, D. and MacPherson, A. (2007) 'Strategic destruction of the North American and European commercial aircraft industry: implications of the system integration business model', Occasional Paper 35. Buffalo, NY: Canada-United States Trade Center.

Renaissance Securities (2006) 'Russian airlines: flying in turbulence', research report, May. London: Renaissance Capital.

Ricupero, Rubens (2003) Press conference to launch *World Investment Report 2003*, 4 September; available at: *www.unctad.org/en/docs* (accessed: 5 May 2008).

Robinson, William I. and Harris, Jerry (2000) 'Towards a global ruling class: globalisation and the transnational capitalist class', *Science and Society*, 64(1): 11–54.

Rodrik, D. (2006) 'What's so special about China's exports?', NBER Working Paper No. 11947. Cambridge, MA: National Bureau of Economic Research.

Ronen, S. and Shenkar, O. (1985) 'Clustering countries on attitudinal dimensions: a review and a synthesis', *Academy of Management Review*, 10(3): 435–54.

Rugman, A. (1996) *The Theory of Multinational Enterprises*. Cheltenham: Edward Elgar.

Rugman, A. (2001) 'The myth of global strategy', *Insight*, 1(1), *AIB Newsletter*, 7(2): 11–14.

Rugman, A. and Cruz, J.D. (2000) *Multinationals at Flagship Firms: Regional Business Networks*. Oxford: Oxford University Press.

Saee, John (2007) 'Intercultural awareness is the key to international business success', *EFMD Global Focus*, June: 58–9.

Saunders, P.C. (2006) 'China's global activism: strategy, drivers and tools', INSS Report. Washington, DC: INSS.

Savage, Mike (2007) 'Media matters for America', October; available at: *http://mediamatters.org/issues_topics/tags/ michael_savage* (accessed: 12 May 2008).

Schott, Peter K. (2007) 'The relative sophistication of Chinese exports', NBER Working Paper No. 12173. Cambridge, MA: National Bureau of Economic Research.

Schwartz, P. (1991) *The Art of the Long View*. New York: Doubleday/Currency.

Schumpeter, J. (1942) *Capitalism, Socialism and Democracy*. New York: Harper & Row.

Sharma, A. (1994) 'Bangalore: the Silicon Valley of India', *Software Today*, October: 84–8.

Silvera, Virginia (2000) 'Embraer and Bombardier disagree over statistics' (translated by Daniel Cooke), *Gazetta Mercantil*, 24 February.

Simons, Robert L. (1992) 'Asea Brown Boveri: the Abacus system', Harvard Business School Case Study No. 9-192-140. Boston, MA: Harvard Business School.

Smith, Adam (1759) *The Theory of Moral Sentiments.*

Smith, Adam (1776) *An Inquiry into the Nature and Causes of the Wealth of Nations.*

Stalk, G. and Hout, T. (1990) *Competing Against Time.* New York: Free Press.

Stigler, George Joseph (1968) *The Organization of Industry.* Homewood, IL: Irwin.

Stirton, K. (2003) 'US multi-industry; commercial aerospace series, part 1; overview and conclusions', *Bernstein Research Call*, 8 October.

Summers, Diana (1996) 'Bespoke jeans for the masses', *Financial Times*, 12 September, p. 13.

Taveres, A.T. (2002) 'Multinational subsidiary evolution and public policy: two tales from the European periphery', *Journal of Industry, Competition and Trade*, 2(3): 195–213.

Taylor, Frederick W. (1911) *The Principles of Scientific Management.* New York: Harper & Row.

Terekhov, A.A. (2001) 'The Russian software industry', *IEEE Software*, December: 98–101.

The Economist (2005) 'The future of Japanese business', *The Economist*, 14 December; available at: *www.economist .com/business/displaystory.cfm?story_id=E1_VPDDTVQ* (accessed: 12 May 2008).

Tian, R.G. (undated) Professor of Business Administration, Erskine College, USA, based on notes from Marketing in the 21st Century; available at: *www.studyoverseas.com/ america/usaed/crosscultural.htm* (accessed: 21 April 2008).

Treacy, Michael and Wiersema, Fred (1993) 'Customer intimacy and other value disciplines', *Harvard Business Review*, January: 84–93.

Tung, R.L. (1984) 'How to negotiate with the Japanese', *California Management Review*, 26(4): 52–77.

Turpin, Andrew (1998) 'Rolls-Royce lands order from BA 777 fleet', *The Scotsman*, 28 September.

UNCTAD (2005) *World Investment Report 2005: Transnational Corporations and the Internationalization of R&D*. New York: United Nations.

UNCTAD (2006) *World Investment Report 2006, FDI from Developing and Transition Economies: Implications for Development*. New York: United Nations.

UNCTAD (2007) *Global Value Chains for Building National Productive Capacities*, Document No. GE.06-52617, February. Geneva: UNCTAD.

Vines, Mike (2007) 'Embraer's rapid ramp-up: the inside story from the Brazilian plane maker', *AV Buyer*, 22 March; available at: *www.avbuyer.com/Articles/Article .asp?Id=770* (accessed: 19 December 2007).

Waples, John (2007) 'The Rock is rapidly becoming a millstone', *Sunday Times*, 2 December; available at: *http://business.timesonline.co.uk/tol/business/columnists/ article2982669.ece* (accessed: 12 May 2008).

Wederspahn, Gary (2000) *Intercultural Services: A Worldwide Buyer's Guide and Sourcebook*. Houston, TX: Gulf Publishing.

Welch, J. (with Welch, S.) (2005) *Winning*. London: HarperCollins Publishers.

Williams, E.E. (1987) *The Emergence of Entrepreneurship in China*. Houston, TX: Jesse H. Jones Graduate School of Administration.

World Bank (2004) 'The Russian lesson: a market economy needs an effective state. Russia's new economic program: does Putinomics mean a slimmed but muscular state?', *Transition Newsletter*, 11(3/4): 3–4.

World Bank (2005) *Overview: World Development Report 2005. A Better Investment Climate for Everyone.* Washington, DC: World Bank.

World Bank (2007) *Country Reports: Doing Business in Brazil.* Washington, DC: World Bank.

World Trade Organization (2004) *World Trade Report 2004: Exploring the Linkage between the Domestic Policy Environment and International Trade.* Geneva: WTO.

World Trade Organization (2005) *World Trade Report 2005: Exploring the Links between Trade, Standards and the WTO.* Geneva: WTO.

Xiao, Ma (2006) 'Self-developed jet to fly maiden trip', *China Daily*, 1 June; available at: *www.chinadaily.com.cn/cndy/2006-06/01/content_605406.htm* (accessed: 24 December 2007).

Yee, A. (2006) 'FDI in India expected to double', FT.com, 28 December; available at: *www.ft.com/cms/s/* (accessed: 5 May 2008).

Zvereva, P. (2007) 'Aerospace industry: defining production tasks', *Russia & CIS Observer*, 3(18); available at: *www.ato.ru/rus/cis/archive/18-2007/aero/aero2/* (accessed: 5 May 2008).

Index